Bloggers

Connecting you to English around the world

1 A1 ▸ A2

Series Editor | **Laura Broadbent**

Project Manager | **Frédéric Chotard**

Author Team
Céline Blanchard, Nathalie Brient,
Lynda Corvé, Virginie Jousset,
Agnès Pihuit-Imbert,
Adeline Wion-Goguillon

You can find all the audios and videos on our free DELTA Augmented app.

| Download the free DELTA Augmented app onto your device | Start picture recognition and scan the **first page of each unit.** | Download files and use them now or save them for later |

Apple and the Apple logo are trademarks of Apple Inc., registered in the US and other countries. App Store is a service mark of Apple Inc. | Google Play and the Google Play logo are trademarks of Google Inc.

1st edition   1 9 8 7 6 5 | 2026 25 24 23 22

All rights reserved. No part of this publication may be reproduced, stored in a retrieval system, or transmitted, in any form or by any means, electronic, mechanical, photocopying, recording, or otherwise, without prior written permission from the publisher.

Delta Publishing, 2020
www.deltapublishing.co.uk

© French edition by Editions Maison des Langues, Paris, France, 2017
© International edition by DELTA Publishing, Ernst Klett Sprachen GmbH, Stuttgart, Germany, 2020

Series Editor: Laura Broadbent, Brighton, UK
Design: Datagroup Int, Timisoara, Romania
Printing and binding: Elanders GmbH, Waiblingen, Germany

ISBN 978-3-12-501202-8

Foreword

Hi there,
Welcome to your book!

I'm Laura. I don't know about you, but I think a great book is made by two teams, the writers and the learners. I'm on the author team and you are on the learner team!

We've worked really hard to make this book fun and interesting. We've put things in that we find fascinating and think you will too. We've also included a lot of our own experiences, which we think you might be going through now.

This means you are learning *real* English. When you take a look at the English school in Unit 1, the uniform, timetable, classrooms, that's how my school was!

In this book, teenagers just like you present the eight units. In each unit, they talk about aspects of their lives in English speaking countries like the United Kingdom and the United States. They also write about things that interest them on a shared blog. That's why this book is called **Bloggers**! You can find their blog posts in the Culture Blog pages in each unit.

Sheena — Tom — Tara — John — Kirstine

And now, you! Here are some tips to help you through this school year:

- ✓ **Take part in class**: Talk and listen as much as you can. Try to speak in English even when it's hard. Also remember, other people will always say things you don't think of!

- ✓ **Respect other people around you**: your teacher and your classmates. We can only learn by making mistakes. Imagine how you'd feel if someone laughed at you, try not to make someone else feel like that.

- ✓ **Ask questions**: If you don't understand something, ask your teacher to explain it in a different way; if you don't agree with something someone says, ask the speaker to explain their reasons; if you don't believe a text, find out who wrote it and think why they have those opinions.

- ✓ At home, take time to revise new things you've learned. There are lots of learning pages at the back of the book to help you. Try different ways to learn and remember things. Have variety and keep your brain fresh!

- ✓ Give yourself time off. You have a lot of exams and stress at the moment but having a rest is really important.

- ✓ Take care of your things: this book, your notebook, pens and pencils. If you keep them in good condition, you can work better.

- ✓ **Final tip**: Keep trying! It takes years to learn a new language, not days. There will be things you find hard but keep trying. That moment when you can do something new will come!

Make Bloggers your own, unique book.
Have a great year with Bloggers!

Table of Contents

	PROJECTS	COMMUNICATION AND GRAMMAR GOALS

Unit 1 — New school, new life

Hi! I'm Sheena from London.

What is the first day of school in England like?

p. 18

MINI CHALLENGE 1
Interview a classmate to find out their new identity.

MINI CHALLENGE 2
Give a welcome speech in your school.

YOUR CHALLENGE
Start to create the class **yearbook**.

⇢ Check your skills WB p. 23

LESSON 1. WHERE ARE YOU FROM?
I can introduce myself to my new class.
- Subject pronouns
- Question words (1)
- The present tense of the verb **to be** (1)
- Talking about likes and dislikes

LESSON 2. WELCOME TO MY SCHOOL!
I can talk about schools in England.
- Articles: **a / an**, **the** and the zero article
- Possessive adjectives (1)
- **there is / this is**

Unit 2 — American family

Hi! I'm Tom from New York.

What are American families like?

p. 30

MINI CHALLENGE 1
Invent the family tree of a celebrity family.

MINI CHALLENGE 2
Create a character and guess your classmates' characters.

YOUR CHALLENGE
Create the family characters for a new American TV series.

⇢ Check your skills WB p. 37

LESSON 1. WE ARE FAMILY!
I can introduce the members of a family.
- The verb **have got** (1)
- The present tense of the verb **to be** (2)
- Possessive adjectives (2)

LESSON 2. HAVE YOU GOT BLUE EYES?
I can describe a physical appearance.
- The verb **have got** (2)
- Asking questions with **be** and **have got**
- Adjective position

REVIEW
- Short answers
- Singular possessive adjectives

Unit 3 — My week

Hi! I'm Tara from Dublin.

What is a normal day like for Irish teenagers?

p. 42

MINI CHALLENGE 1
Present your perfect timetable for a day.

MINI CHALLENGE 2
Do a survey about the class's activities outside school.

YOUR CHALLENGE
Present a slideshow for a typical day for Tara.

⇢ Check your skills WB p. 51

LESSON 1. WAKE UP!
I can talk about what I do everyday and how I spend my time.
- The present simple (1)
- Time expressions (1)

LESSON 2. I play Gaelic football
I can talk about my hobbies.
- Adverbs of frequency (1)
- Question words (2)
- Questions and short answers

REVIEW
- **like / love / hate** + verb-**ing** / noun or noun phrase / **to** + verb root
- The verb **have got**

Unit 4 — Home, sweet home

Hi! I'm John from Los Angeles.

What are houses and home life like in American cartoons?

p. 54

MINI CHALLENGE 1
Design a short advert to sell a house.

MINI CHALLENGE 2
Invent crazy home rules.

YOUR CHALLENGE
Imagine an unusual house and family for Tim Burton's next film.

⇢ Check your skills WB p. 65

LESSON 1. WELCOME TO MY HOUSE!
I can describe an American house.
- **there is / there are**
- The possessive ('s)
- The negative and questions form of **have got** (3)
- **how many**

LESSON 2. HOME RULES
I can talk about my room and housework.
- Object pronouns
- Obligation and prohibition

REVIEW
- **there is**

Bloggers 1

LEXICAL AND PHONOLOGICAL GOALS	CROSS-CULTURAL LESSONS	CULTURAL GOALS
VOCABULARY • Languages, countries and nationalities • Leisure activities (1) • Different places in school • Prepositions of place (1) **REVIEW** • Numbers **PRONUNCIATION** • Sentence stress • Different ways of pronouncing **"th"**	**ARTISTIC AND CULTURAL EDUCATION** • The Hindu Diwali festival • Indian food • Indian political journalist Anushka Asthana **CITIZENSHIP** • Respect for cultural diversity 	• School in England • Introducing yourself • Introducing your classmates • Different countries and nationalities • London, multicultural city
VOCABULARY • Family members • Physical description **REVIEW** • Colours **PRONUNCIATION** • The contracted forms of **have got** and **has got** • The sound /ɪ/ and the diphthong /aɪ/	**ARTISTIC AND CULTURAL EDUCATION** • Family in art: **Freedom from Want**, by Norman Rockwell **CITIZENSHIP** • Different types of family 	• Talking about yourself • Some famous fictional American families • New York City (USA) • Thanksgiving • **Little Women**, by Louisa May Alcott, and **Going and Coming**, by Norman Rockwell
VOCABULARY • Daily activities • School material • Leisure activities (2) **REVIEW** • Leisure activities • The days of the week **PRONUNCIATION** • **"-s"** and **"-es"** in the third-person singular • Sentence stress • How to pronounce **"ea"**	**ARTISTIC AND CULTURAL EDUCATION** • Gaelic football • Irish dance **HEALTH EDUCATION** • Body and mind in harmony 	• Everyday life in an Irish school • Likes and habits • Typical Irish activities • Dublin city
VOCABULARY • Rooms in the house • Furniture • Prepositions of place (2) • Housework • Some leisure activities (3) **REVIEW** • Colours • The family • Everyday activities **PRONUNCIATION** • The pronunciation of **"'s"** • **there is / there are** and **there isn't / there aren't**	**ARTISTIC AND CULTURAL EDUCATION** • Houses in Tim Burton's films **CITIZENSHIP** • Sharing housework between men and women 	• American homes • Family life at home • The city of Los Angeles • The universe of film-maker Tim Burton

Table of Contents

	PROJECTS	COMMUNICATION AND GRAMMAR GOALS
Unit 5 **Looking good!** *Hi! This is Sheena from London.* How do London teenagers dress and where do they shop? p. 66	**MINI CHALLENGE 1** Write an article about fashion and teenagers for a magazine. **MINI CHALLENGE 2** Act out a scene in a clothes shop in London. **YOUR CHALLENGE** Create a new collection of school uniforms for Marks & Spencer and present it. ⇢ Check your skills WB p. 81	**LESSON 1. What are you wearing?** I can talk about outfits. • The auxiliary verb **can** • The present form of **to be** + verb + -ing (present continuous) **LESSON 2. A shopping day** I learn to express myself in a shop. • How much? • Expressing desires (**would like**) • Expressing agreement and disagreement • Prices **REVIEW** • Possessive adjectives • **like** / **love** / **hate** + verb-**ing** / noun or noun phrase / **to** + verb
Unit 6 **Let's play ball!** *Hi! This is John from Los Angeles.* Do they play the same sports in the United States as we do? p. 78	**MINI CHALLENGE 1** Invent a new American sport for a competition. **MINI CHALLENGE 2** Promote your favourite sports club. **YOUR CHALLENGE** Create a poster to promote a new American sport. ⇢ Check your skills WB p. 97	**LESSON 1. You mustn't kick the ball!** I can talk about typical American sports. • need / need to **LESSON 2. Becoming a champ** I can talk about sporting talent and diets for athletes. • can/can't • Degrees of ability • Qualifying adverbs • Coordinating conjunctions **REVIEW** • **like** / **love** / **hate** + verb + -**ing** / noun or noun phrase / **to** + verb root • **must** / **mustn't**
Unit 7 **New York, New York** *Hi! This is Tom from New York.* What defines New York city? p. 90 	**MINI CHALLENGE 1** Describe a tourist experience for a tourist guide. **MINI CHALLENGE 2** Imagine the story of an immigrant who is going to the USA. **YOUR CHALLENGE** Talk about your trip to New York… playing with dice! ⇢ Check your skills WB p. 111	**LESSON 1. Come to NYC!** I can describe my trip to Manhattan. • The past simple (1) **LESSON 2. The island of hope** I discover the history of Ellis Island. • The past simple (2) • Time markers for the past tense **REVIEW** • Saying the time • there is / there are • would like to • must
Unit 8 **A trip to Scotland** *Hi! I'm Kirstine from Glasgow.* What are the main attractions in Scotland? p. 102 	**MINI CHALLENGE 1** Organise a two-day tourist route. **MINI CHALLENGE 2** Organise a sightseeing day in Glasgow. **YOUR CHALLENGE** Organise a tourist route around Scotland. ⇢ Check your skills WB p. 127	**LESSON 1. We'll visit Loch Ness!** I can talk about tourist routes and the weather in Scotland. • will + verb **LESSON 2. Let's go to Glasgow!** I can organise holiday activities in Glasgow. • The first conditional (if… will) • Time expressions (2) • Making suggestions **REVIEW** • Would like to • There is / there are • Can

| EXERCISES p. 114 | READING p. 122 | LEARNING STRATEGIES p. 130

LEXICAL AND PHONOLOGICAL GOALS	CROSS-CULTURAL LESSONS	CULTURAL GOALS
VOCABULARY • Clothes and accessories • The seasons • Shopping and shops • Numbers **REVIEW** • The colours • Physical description **PRONUNCIATION** • The sound /ə/ • Lengthening of vowels before an "r"	**ARTISTIC AND CULTURAL EDUCATION** • London fashion and the designer Stella McCartney **CITIZENSHIP** • School uniforms: for or against? 	• Dressing styles • Clothes shopping • Dress sense • London and its markets: Brick Lane, Oxford Street… • School uniforms in England
VOCABULARY • Sports • Sports equipment • Adjectives that express ability and skills • Food and diet **REVIEW** • Leisure activities **PRONUNCIATION** • How to pronounce **can** and **can't**	**ARTISTIC AND CULTURAL EDUCATION** • Baseball, a typical American sport • The baseball legend Ernie Banks **CITIZENSHIP** • Fair play 	• Sport and diet • Individual sports • Some famous North American sporting personalities • Some typical North American sports: curling, baseball, ice hockey
VOCABULARY • Places in town • Qualifying adjectives • Travel and feelings • Verbs in the past **REVIEW** • Shops and places in town **PRONUNCIATION** • The pronunciation of "-ed"	**ARTISTIC AND CULTURAL EDUCATION** • Skyscrapers in Manhattan **CITIZENSHIP** • The Melting Pot 	• Expressing feelings • **At Ellis Island: a History in Many Voices**, by Louise Peacock • New York city and its most famous buildings • Some immigrants' journeys to the United States
VOCABULARY • Outdoor activities • Landscapes • The weather • Different places in town • Tourist activities • Means of transport **PRONUNCIATION** • The pronunciation of **will** • Intonation in sentences	**ARTISTIC AND CULTURAL EDUCATION** • Two Scottish legends **CITIZENSHIP** • Planet-friendly means of transport 	• Organisation of leisure activities • The city of Glasgow • Some Scottish tourist spots • The Loch Ness monster and the legend of the salmon and the ring

Bloggers 1

Discover Bloggers

What do the icons in your Student's Book mean?

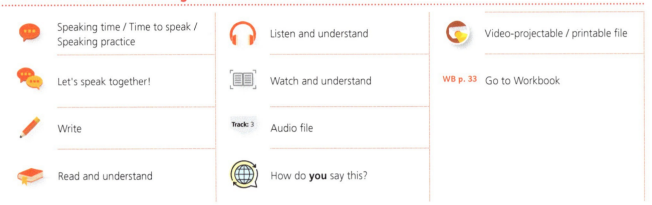

💬 Speaking time / Time to speak / Speaking practice	🎧 Listen and understand	Video-projectable / printable file
💬💬 Let's speak together!	📖 Watch and understand	WB p. 33 Go to Workbook
✏️ Write	Track: 3 Audio file	
📕 Read and understand	🌐 How do **you** say this?	

How does each unit work?

The opening double page

The main character of the unit, who presents their city and the topic that you're going to be looking at.

The objectives of the unit and your challenge! This is the task that you're asked to carry out, and which we're sure you'll be able to do.

A simple question about a specific aspect of the English-speaking world. The unit will equip you with the tools you need to respond.

Two activities to familiarise you with the subject and revise what you've learned.

A vlog by the teenager in the unit.

The two lessons

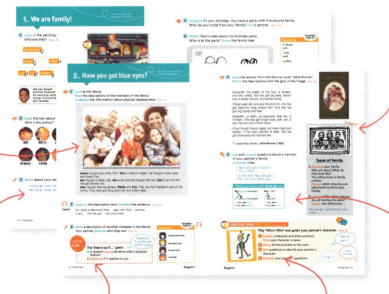

All kinds of **documents** (texts, videos, recordings, images…), **authentic** and always interesting!

Need help to express yourself? Use the prompts or the **examples in blue.**

Games, because you always learn better when you're having fun!

A mini challenge to put what you've learned into practice and train you up for the final **challenge.**

Reflection to help prepare you **to become a citizen of the world…** in English, of course!

The essential **grammar** and **vocabulary** you need to remember.

8 eight   Bloggers 1

My grammar / My vocabulary

Simple explanations and exercises for each grammar point seen in the unit.

Make the **Workbook** your friend; it'll train you to speak English like a native!

A mind map to visualise all the key vocabulary in the unit. Words are easier to memorise when they're grouped in a logical, visual way!

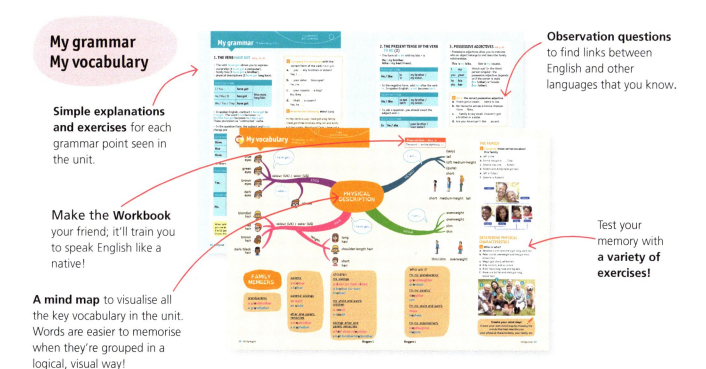

Observation questions to find links between English and other languages that you know.

Test your memory with **a variety of exercises!**

The Culture Blog

The blog by the main character of the unit and all the other bloggers in the coursebook.
Read their articles to get into the topic of each unit… then start the creative phase!

Your challenge

Your mission! All the stages are there in detail, and the examples are there to help you. You have all the cards in your hand to succeed!

What else is there in your Student's Book?

There are pages...

… about phonetics. … about learning strategies. … of exercises. … of texts to read.

 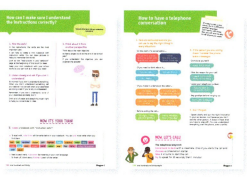  

Bloggers 1 · nine 9

And what's so special about the Workbook?

To complement the lessons

Different ways to do each activity, **one that's more challenging, and one with more support!**

The documents in your Student's Book can be circled, highlighted or underlined as much as you want!

Steps to reflect on the language and work out the grammar rules for **yourself.**

Grids to complete for each mini challenge so you can evaluate your own work… as well as that of your classmates!

Learning strategies for you to reflect on your learning, and work out which techniques work best for you.

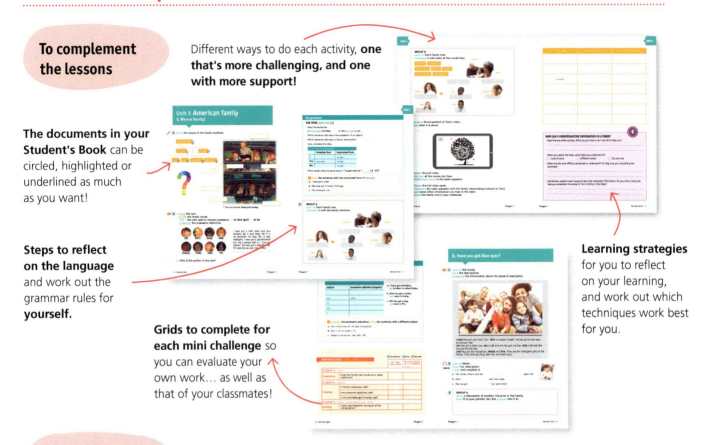

To memorise your vocabulary

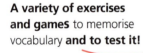

A variety of exercises and games to memorise vocabulary **and to test it!**

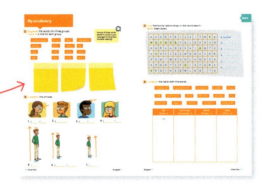

To improve your pronunciation

Activities to train you to recognise and to pronounce **the sounds, the intonation and the rhythm of English.**

To prepare you for assessment

Five training activities to help you on assessment day.

Bookquest

Let's play! Here are some questions about your Student's Book. Answer them as fast as you can with a classmate. The first pair to finish are the winners!

The first pages of the Student's Book →

A How many units are there in the Student's Book?

B Why is it called **Bloggers**?

C What's the name of the main character in Unit 2?

Unit 2 **American family**

D Which cities in the English-speaking world will you find out about? Find at least four, from two different countries!

Meet the **Bloggers**

← The units

F How many lessons are there in a unit?

COMMUNICATION AND GRAMMAR OBJECTIVES

E What will you be able to do in English in this course? Find at least five different things!

G What does the box below refer to on the first page of each unit?

Your challenge Start to create the class yearbook.

I What's the name of the diagram that you find on the **My vocabulary** pages? What is it for?

J What's the link between the bloggers and the **Culture Blog** page?

H What can you find in the **My grammar** section?

I understand and I practice.

My grammar → Exercises p. 114

K What type of activity does the icon below represent?

LET'S PLAY...

← Additional resources in the coursebook

N Where can you find extra grammar exercises?

M What should you do when you see this note? **WB p. 24**

L In the **Vocabulary** tables, why are some letters in orange?

tall
m**e**dium-height
short

O How many Learning Strategies files can you consult if you need guidance? Say at least four of the topics!

How to have a telephone conversation

P What can you find after page 130?

Well done! Your Student's Book has no secrets for you! You can use it through the whole course... or you can look through the pages whenever you want.

Bloggers 1   eleven **11**

Meet the Bloggers

Here are the five bloggers you're going to meet in this book. They are from different English-speaking countries. They all contribute to the Culture Blog, a collaborative blog where they write about what they're interested in.
Let's meet them!

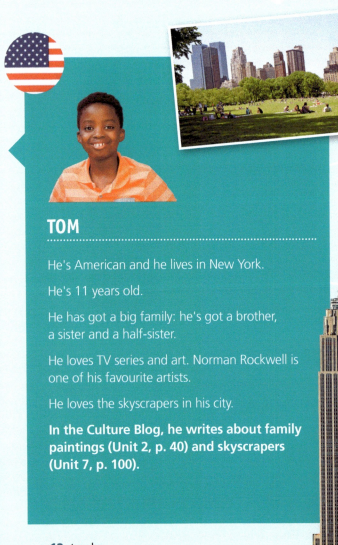

TOM

He's American and he lives in New York.

He's 11 years old.

He has got a big family: he's got a brother, a sister and a half-sister.

He loves TV series and art. Norman Rockwell is one of his favourite artists.

He loves the skyscrapers in his city.

In the Culture Blog, he writes about family paintings (Unit 2, p. 40) and skyscrapers (Unit 7, p. 100).

SHEENA

She's British, but her family comes from India.

She's 11 years old.

She's in Year 7 at an international school near London.

She loves sports but she doesn't like playing video games, and she hates cooking.

She likes design and fashion, too. Stella McCartney is one of her favourite designers.

In the Culture Blog, she writes about multicultural London (Unit 1, p. 28) and fashion (Unit 5, p. 76).

TARA

She's from Dublin, Ireland.

She's 11 years old.

She's in the sixth year at school, and her favourite subjects are art and drama. She doesn't like business studies.

In her free time, she does Irish dancing and she likes surfing the Net at home.

In the Culture Blog, she writes about two very Irish activities (Unit 3, p. 52).

KIRSTINE

She lives in Glasgow, Scotland.

She's 11 and a half.

She likes hiking in the mountains, especially the Highlands in the north of Scotland.

She loves telling myths and legends, like the one about Nessie, the Loch Ness monster.

In the Culture Blog, she writes about Scottish myths and legends (Unit 8, p. 112).

JOHN

He's from Los Angeles, California.

He has got a big house with a big garden. He has got a brother and a sister.

He loves cinema, especially the films by Tim Burton, and baseball. The Los Angeles Dodgers are his favourite team.

In the Culture Blog, he writes about Tim Burton's houses in films (Unit 4, p. 64) and baseball (Unit 6, p. 88).

LET'S GO!

Read the comic strips and **memorise** them.
Act them **out** with a partner! WB p. 5

2. Let's celebrate!

I can talk about the days, months and national celebrations in the English-speaking world.

January

- 1st New Year's Day
- 26th Australia Day

February

- 6th Waitangi Day (New Zealand)
- 14th Valentine's Day

March

 spring

- 1st St David's Day (Wales)
- 17th St Patrick's Day (Ireland)

April

- 21st The Queen's birthday (England)
- 23rd St George's Day (England)
- 27th Freedom Day (South Africa)

May

- 1st Labor Day (USA) / May Day (UK)
- 25th Africa Day

June

 summer

On a Saturday

Trooping the Colour (England)

16 sixteen

Bloggers 1

July

- 1st — Canada Day
- 4th — Independence Day (USA)

August

- 15th — Independence Day (India)

September

autumn / fall

- 11th — Patriot Day (USA)

October

- 31st — Halloween

November

- 5th — Guy Fawkes' Night (England)
- The 4th Thursday — Thanksgiving (USA)
- 30th — St Andrew's Day (Scotland)

December

winter

- 25th — Christmas
- 26th — Boxing Day
- 31st — New Year's Eve

LET'S GO!

Create a calendar for your English class. Take it in turns to ask and answer about your birthdays and write it on the calendar. Now we can celebrate birthdays in class! WB p. 6

Unit 1
New school, new life

How do they spend the first day of school in England?

▸ **In this unit we are going to…**
- introduce ourselves to our new classmates.
- talk about schools in England.
- discover the wealth of diversity in multicultural London.
- talk about cultural diversity.

Your challenge
Create the class yearbook.

Hi, I am **SHEENA**, from London (UK). I'm English, but my family is from India. In this unit you will learn about the first day of school in Year 7 in England.

↑ Piccadilly Circus, London

↑ Sheena's vlog

LET'S GO!

1 **Listen to** Sheena's conversation. **Complete** the sentences:
  a. It's Sheena's first...
  b. In the school, there is...

Track: 01

2 **Look** at the picture of Sheena's video. What can you see? **Tell** a partner.

1. Where are you from?

> I can introduce myself to my new classmates.

1 **Listen** to three introductions and **match** them with an illustration. **Read** three more introductions. **Match** them with the correct illustrations. WB p. 8

Track: 02

a. My name is Sheena. I am British. I am nearly twelve.
b. I am Eva. I'm from Spain and I am eleven years old.
c. We are Carl and Hans. We are German. We're eleven.

Write an introduction for the two remaining characters.

Did you know?
English people are from England. British people are from the United Kingdom (England + Scotland + Wales + Northern Ireland).

2 In Sheena's school, there is a Welcome Club. **Listen to** the dialogue and **complete** the forms. WB p. 9

Track: 03

Vocabulary
Vocabulary track: 01

COUNTRIES	NATIONALITIES
Belgium	Belgian
China	Chinese
France	French
Germany	German
India	Indian
Spain	Spanish
The USA	American
The United Kingdom	British

Question words
What is your name?
How old are you?
When is your birthday?
Where are you from?
What is your nationality?
Where do you live?
What languages do you speak?

The present tense of the verb "to be"
I am English. / I am not English.
We are English. / We are not English.

Are you English?
→ Yes, I am. / Yes, we are.
→ No, I am not. / No, we are not.

LAST NAME:
AGE:
BIRTHDAY:
NATIONALITY:
LANGUAGES SPOKEN:

REGISTRATION FORM

FIRST NAME:
LAST NAME:
AGE:
BIRTHDAY:
NATIONALITY:
LANGUAGES SPOKEN:

LET'S PLAY...

A ball game (group work)
1. **Take** a ball and **introduce** yourself: say your name, your age, your nationality and the languages you speak.
2. **Pass** the ball to a person in the group.

My name is Sara. I am eleven...

3 **Watch** Sheena's video about her first day at school and new friends. **Take notes** about their favourite activities. **WB p. 12** **Compare** your notes with your classmate. And you? What do you do in your free time? **Tell** your partner.

I love swimming.

↑ Sheena's vlog

Vocabulary — Vocabulary track: 02

- to cook
- to cycle
- to go on the computer
- to play cricket / football
- to play in the garden
- to play video games
- to read
- to swim
- to watch TV
- to write

4 **Read** Sheena's section in the school yearbook. **Complete** your own profile in your notebook.

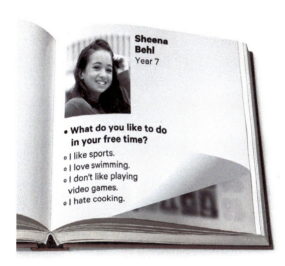

Did you know?

A yearbook, is a book published annually to record and celebrate the past year at a school.

Expressing likes and dislikes

like / love / hate + to + infinitive verb
I like to swim.

like / love / hate + verb-ing
I like swimming.

like / love / hate + noun / nominal group
I like sports.
I like science fiction films.

I don't like + to + infinitive
            + verb-ing
            + noun / nominal group

MINI CHALLENGE: A NEW IDENTITY (pair work)

It's the first day at your new school. You play a game to get to know each other. WB p. 13

1 Create a new identity for yourself: a new name, an age, a birthday, a nationality, a place of residence and the language(s) you speak.

2 Think about what you like or don't like to do in your free time.

3 Ask and **answer** questions.

4 Complete your classmate's card.

I can talk about schools.

2. Welcome to my school!

1 **Look** at the picture. What do you think the video is about? Why? **Tell** a partner.

↑ Sheena's vlog

2 **Watch** the video and **write** the names next to what Eva's friends think. Two phrases are true about one person. **WB p. 14**

Sheena   Jae   Raphael   Eva

a. I don't like reading in English because it is difficult and I don't know all the words.

b. I like London because it's so international, but I miss my friends.

c. I like our house in England because we've got a garden. I love playing in the garden.

d. I love the class because we play video games and explain our opinions.

CITIZENSHIP

We all smile

1. **Look at** the poster. **Find** the slogan.

2. **Rephrase** the message.
We come from different countries but...

↑ Rimidesigns, **We All Smile in The Same Language**

3 **Work** in groups. **Discuss** the questions.

a. Where are you from? Where is your family from?
b. What do you think of reading in another language? Is it difficult/easy/important?
c. Do you have friends from different countries?
d. What do you think are the positive/negatives about having friends from different countries?
e. Do you like the IT class? Why (not)?

4 **Complete** the table with the correct activities. **Use** the sentence starters to write sentences.

Sheena	Eva	Raphael	Jae

Sheena doesn't like ...
Jae likes ...

Bloggers 1

5 **Tell** your partner about your first day at school. WB p. 15

"We have assembly and I go to the classroom. I sit next to …"

6 **Look** at the plan of the school. Four room names are missing.
Watch the video again and **write** the missing rooms in the correct places.
Complete Sheena's sentences.

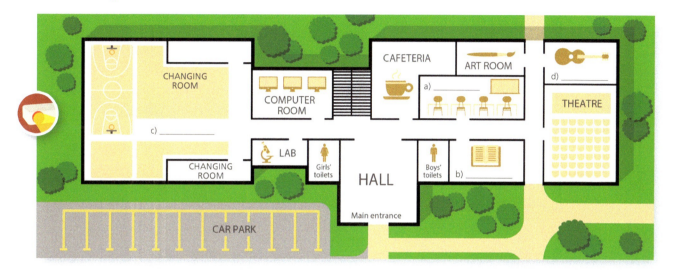

This is my school.
a. The cafeteria is next to the … and the … .
b. There is a lab opposite the … .
c. The … is between the girls' toilets and the boys' toilets.
d. The … is opposite the music room.

Articles
There is a library in our school.
This is the library where I study.

Vocabulary
Vocabulary track: 03

near / next to   between   opposite

 LET'S PLAY…

Find the room (pair work)
1. **Choose** a place in the school.
2. **Explain** where it is.
3. Your partner **guesses**.

It's a small room next to the library. What is it?

 MINI CHALLENGE: YOUR SCHOOL

It's Open Day in your school.
Give the welcome speech. WB p. 19

1 **Decide** the name, location and number of students in your school.
2 **Complete** a school plan.
3 **Describe** your new school!

I go to a High School in Plymouth. We are over…

This is the hall. There is a… between the library and the…

Bloggers 1   twenty-three **23**

My grammar → Exercises p. 114

I understand and I practise.

1. SUBJECT PRONOUNS

I	I am Sheena.
you	You are 11 years old.
he / she	She is English.
it	It is my school.
we	We go to a great school.
they	They are my friends.

> In English, **you** refers both to the second-person singular and the second-person plural. Does the same thing happen in other languages?

2. QUESTION WORDS (1) WB p. 10

Question words are at the beginning of a question. Use them to ask questions about:

What...? a thing, a situation, a person's name, nationality, likes, dislikes...
What sport do you like?

When...? a date / time
When does school start?

Where...? place
Where is the canteen?

Where ...from? origin of a person or thing
Where are you from?

Who...? person
Who is the teacher?

How old ...? age
How old are you?

> Notice! 4 of the question words start with 'wh-'

1 Use these words to create questions. Then answer them. Pay attention to capital letters and punctuation!
a. name what is your
b. old you are how
c. are from where you
d. birthday when your is
e. live where you do
f. nationality what your is
g. speak you languages what do

3. THE PRESENT TENSE OF THE VERB TO BE (1) WB p. 8

- **To be** is a verb that can be used to express...
- identity: I **am** Sarah.
- age: I **am** eleven.
- place of origin: I **am** from the USA.
- nationality: I **am** American.

POSITIVE FORM		
I	am	from Scotland.
You / We	are	

- In spoken English, the first letter of the verb **to be** is often replaced by an apostrophe.
I am = <u>I'm</u> Sarah
you are = <u>You're</u> 11 years old
she is / he is = <u>She's / He's</u> English.
it is = <u>It's</u> my school.
we are = <u>We're</u> Scottish.
they are = <u>They're</u> my teachers.

These are called **contracted** verbs.

I**'m** Sarah.
We**'re** from the USA.

- In the question form of the verb, the subject and the verb are inverted.

QUESTION FORM		
Am	I	eleven?
Are	you / we	Chinese?

- In the negative form, **not** follows the verb **to be**.

NEGATIVE FORM			
I	am	not	German.
You / We	are		from London.

- In spoken English, the negative form is often contracted: **I am not** becomes **I'm not** and **you/we are not** becomes **you/we aren't**.

I**'m not** Sarah.
We**'re not** from the USA.

- In short positive answers, verbs are not contracted.

SHORT POSITIVE ANSWERS	
Yes,	I am. / we are.
SHORT POSITIVE ANSWERS	
No,	I'm not. / we aren't.

2 Complete the conversation. **Use** contracted forms.

Sharon: Hi!
Paolo: Hi! What's your name?
S: My name's Sharon Cooper. And you?
P: ..... Paolo Ramirez. How old ....?
S: ..... 11.
P: That's funny. ..... both 11!
S: Where are ..... from?
P: Guess!
S: .... Italian?
P: Yes, ... And you?
S: ..... from England.

Pronunciation → WB p. 22

Different ways of pronouncing "th"
Sentence stress

4. LIKES AND DISLIKES WB p. 13

You can use different verbs to talk about what you like or dislike.

 love
 like
 don't like
 hate

When you talk about he/she/it add an **-s** onto the verb.
Sheena **likes** cycling.
In the negative form, the auxiliary **do** changes to **does**.
Sheena **doesn't** like maths.

Use verb + ing to talk about the experience of an action
I like swimming fast.

Use verb + to + infinitive to talk about a habit
I like to run before school.

3 Talk about what Sheena likes and dislikes (or hates). What do you and Sheena have in common?

5. ARTICLES: A / AN, THE AND THE ZERO ARTICLE WB p. 17

Articles provide us with information about noun.

• **The** is used to talk about something that has already been mentioned, or something that everyone knows.
   This is **the** cafeteria.
   The art room is quite big.

• **A / an** are used to refer to something that has not yet been mentioned. The article **a** becomes **an** when used in front of a noun that starts with a vowel sound.
   There is **a** lab and **an** art room in my school.

• The zero article is used to talk about something in general terms.
   I love Ø team sports. / I hate Ø classical dance.

Be careful! When talking about something in general terms in English, you do not use an article (Ø = zero article). But what happens in your language when you talk about something in general?

6. POSSESSIVE ADJECTIVES WB p. 19

Adjectives are used to describe a noun. Possessive adjectives show the relationship between a noun and a person.

I	my
you	your
we	our

This is **my** school.

This is **your** school.

This is **our** school.

4 Complete the sentence with the correct possessive adjective.
Hi! ..... name is Peter, and this is ..... friend Alex. We are eleven. We love playing football on ..... school team. And you? What's ..... name?

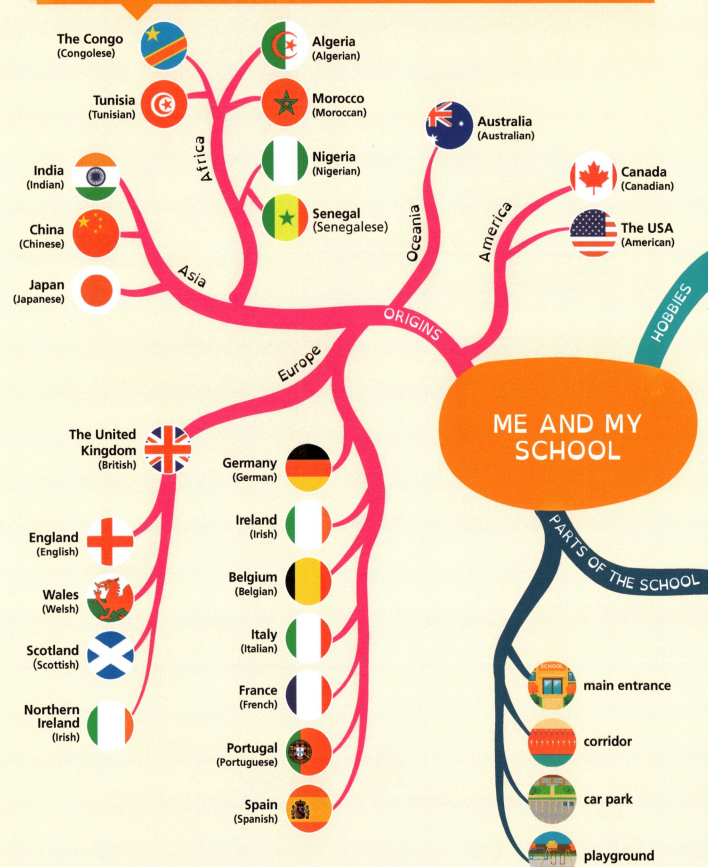

COUNTRIES, NATIONALITIES AND LANGUAGES

1 **Look** at the flags to **complete** the sentences below.

a. Hi, I am Christian. I'm from .... . I live in Melbourne.
b. My name is Petra. I live in Venice. I am .... .
c. Hello! I am Joshua. I'm from .... . I speak .... and English.
d. I am Jean. I live in Paris but I am not .... . I am from .... . I speak .... and English.
e. Hello everybody. My name is Said. I'm .... but I live in .... . I speak Arabic and .... .

2 **Find** the odd one out. **Explain** your answers to your partner.

a. The USA | The United Kingdom | Canada
b. Australia | Portugal | Wales
c. Belgium | Germany | France
d. Italian | Portuguese | Chinese

DIFFERENT PLACES AT SCHOOL

3 **Match** each activity with a place at school.

a. We learn to play the piano in the .... .
b. We play basketball and badminton in the .... .
c. We learn digital skills in the .... .
d. We have lunch in the .... .
e. We borrow books from the .... .
f. We make and then paint our creations in the .... .
g. We have drama lessons in the .... .

Create your mind map!
Create your own mind map by choosing the words that you would use to describe yourself (country, nationality, languages, hobbies) and your school.

http://www.deltapublishing.co.uk/culture-blog

 Today I'm writing about Indian culture in London.

 ARTISTIC AND CULTURAL EDUCATION

MULTICULTURAL LONDON: INDIA

DIWALI

In Autumn, British Indians in London celebrate the festival of Diwali, with music and dance. It's called 'the festival of lights'. It is one of the major festivals of Hinduism. It represents the victory of light over darkness, good over evil, knowledge over ignorance, and hope over despair.

INDIAN FOOD

London is a very diverse city. People come from Europe, Africa and Asia to live in the city. Many people come from India or Pakistan. In London you can eat delicious Indian food like chicken tikka masala. It is a spicy dish that contains chicken, spices and yoghurt. Yummy!

↑ chicken tikka masala

ANUSHKA ASTHANA

Anushka Asthana is a political journalist and newsreader. Her parents are from India and she was born in Scunthorpe, North England. She studied economics at Cambridge University and has reported for a main English newspaper, *The Times*, and *Sky News*. She now lives in London and is a political editor. If you want to know anything about politics, ask Anushka!

Other Posts:
- Family Paintings
- Two Very Irish Acivities
- Tim Burton's Houses
- London Fashion Design
- I Love Baseball
- New York Skyscrapers
- Scottish Legends

Contributors:

 Sheena

 Tom

 Tara

 John

 Kirstine

YOUR TURN!

1 **Go** on the internet.
  Find international festivals in London. What culture do they celebrate?

YOU ARE AN ARTIST!
Create a poster about multicultural London (festivals, areas, food, artists) in groups.

28 twenty-eight

Your challenge

CREATE A CLASS YEARBOOK

It's your first day in a new school with new classmates. Start the yearbook for your class.

1. **Write** a short introduction of yourself: name, age, birthday, nationality, languages you speak, hobbies, likes and dislikes, etc.
2. **Write** a brief introduction of the school: name, location, number of students, different parts...
3. **Take a photo** of yourself and of the different parts of your school.
4. **Create** a page with personal information and another one with the information about the school.
5. **Collect** all the pages to start a yearbook. You will complete it as a class during the year.
6. **Take a class vote** for the best description of the school.

↓ **Digital alternative**
Film your presentations, then save them. You will be able to watch them again in your last year of school.

Welcome to my school in Versailles!
There are 900 students.
In our school, there is a science lab, a big gym and a beautiful library.

My name's Laura Martin.
I'm eleven.
I'm in Year 7.

I like playing football.
I love cooking.
I don't like playing video games.

To show you have completed this challenge, mark your progress in this unit on the **CHECK YOUR SKILLS** section of your Workbook (p. 23).

Unit 2
American family

What are American families like?

→ **In this unit, we are going to...**
- introduce family members.
- describe people's physical characteristics.
- discover American artists.
- talk about different types of families.

Your challenge
Create the family characters for a new American television series.

Hi, I'm **TOM**, from New York (USA). In this unit you will learn about American families.

↑ Tom's family

LET'S GO!

1. **Look at** the pictures and the video still. What do you think this unit is about?

2. What do you know about New York? **Make** a list of things with your group.

thirty-one **31**

1. We are family!

I can introduce the members of a family.

1 Look at the painting. Who are they? **WB p. 24**

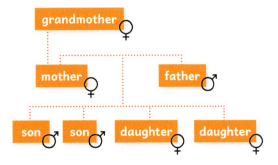

Did you know?
Norman Rockwell (1894-1978) was an American artist. He painted scenes of American people and families.

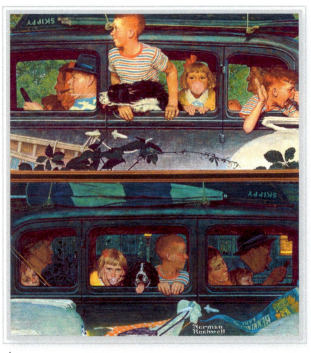

↑ Norman Rockwell, **Going and Coming** (1947)

2 Read the text about this family. Who is the author? **WB p. 24**

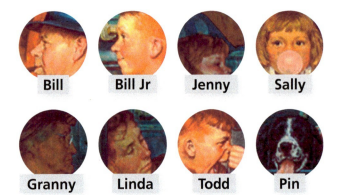

I have got a little sister and two brothers, Bill Jr and Todd. Bill Jr is my favourite! His dog, Pin, is very intelligent. I have got a grandmother
5 too, she is always with us. I love my grandma! We have got a beautiful car. Pin loves the car and I love it too!

Vocabulary — Vocabulary track: 04

mother + father = parents
grandmother + grandfather = grandparents

son + daughter = children
brother
sister

stepfather
stepmother
stepbrother / half-brother
stepsister / half-sister

The verbs have got and to be

I **have got** / I**'ve got** a sister.
We **have got** / We**'ve got** a beautiful car.
She **is** always with us. / She**'s** always with us.

3 Write about your real or fictional family.

I have got one / two...
My sister loves animals...

Pronunciation → WB p. 36
The sound /ɪ/ and the diphthong /aɪ/

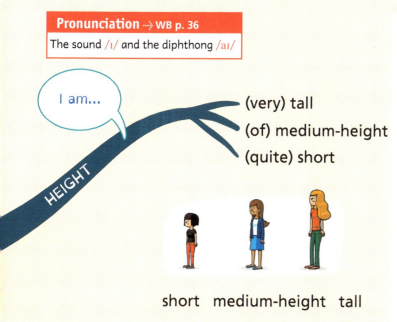

HEIGHT — I am...
- (very) tall
- (of) medium-height
- (quite) short

short   medium-height   tall

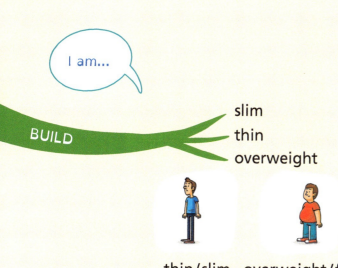

BUILD — I am...
- slim
- thin
- overweight

thin/slim   overweight/fat

Who am I?

I'm my grandparents'
granddaughter
grandson

I'm my parents'
daughter
son

I'm my uncle and aunt's
niece
nephew

I'm my stepmother's
stepdaughter
stepson

THE FAMILY

1 Complete these sentences about this family.
a. Jeff is the .... .
b. Emma has got a .... , Toby.
c. Edwina has one .... , Robert.
d. Robert and Andy have got two .... .
e. Jeff is Toby's .... .
f. Edwina is Robert's .... .

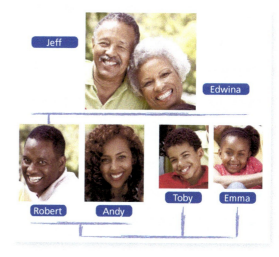

DESCRIBING PHYSICAL CHARACTERISTICS

2 Who is who?
a. Natasha and Sara have got long, dark hair.
b. Peter has got two children and he's got brown hair.
c. Meg's got short, white hair.
d. Billy is short, and he's got short, brown hair.
e. John is tall and he's got short, white hair.

Create your mind map!
Create your own mind map by choosing the words that best describe you: your physical characteristics, your family, etc.

Bloggers 1   thirty-nine 39

Today I'm writing about a family painting by a great artist from the state of Massachusetts.

ARTISTIC AND CULTURAL EDUCATION

FAMILY PAINTINGS

NORMAN ROCKWELL

This is a famous representation of Thanksgiving, by the artist Norman Rockwell. He paints scenes of American life. He has got a realistic style.

Thanksgiving is a traditional family celebration in the USA. In the painting, you can see a grandmother and a grandfather serving a meal to a large family. Everybody is happy and they are smiling.

↑ **Freedom from Want** (1943)

Other Posts:
- Multicultural London: India
- Two Very Irish Activities
- Tim Burton's Houses
- London Fashion Design
- I Love Baseball
- New York Skyscrapers
- Scottish Legends

Contributors:

 Sheena

 Tom

 Tara

 John

 Kirstine

YOUR TURN!

1. **Read** the text. **Look at** the painting. What do you like about the painting? How does it make you feel?
2. **Imagine** you are a member of this family. **Describe** your family to your partner.

YOU ARE AN ARTIST!
Look for a parody of this painting on the Internet.
Invent your own parody with photos of your family and friends.

Your challenge

CREATE THE CHARACTERS FOR A NEW AMERICAN TV SERIES

You are a TV scriptwriter for a new American comedy series.

1. **Think about** the characters and **draw** the family tree.
2. **Write** a description for each member of the family.
3. **Think about** a title for your series.
4. **Present** your characters. You can use pictures or drawings.
5. The class **chooses** the funniest family.

↓ **Digital alternative**
You can create a slideshow to introduce the members of the family and the title of the TV series.

This is Sally Dog. She's got a sister, Molly Dog, and a brother, Mike Dog. She's got brown eyes and a big nose. She loves reading!

And he's Dad Dog. His wife is Mum Dog. He's tall and thin. He's got green eyes and white hair. He loves computers.

Dog family

To show you have completed this challenge, mark your progress in this unit on the **CHECK YOUR SKILLS** section of your Workbook (p. 37).

Unit 3
My week

What is a normal day like for Irish teenagers?

→ **In this unit, we are going to...**
- talk about our everyday activities and how we spend our time.
- talk about our hobbies.
- discover two typically Irish activities.
- talk about physical and mental health.

Your challenge
Present a slideshow of your typical day.

I'm **TARA**, from Dublin (Ireland). In this unit you will learn about the everyday life of Irish students.

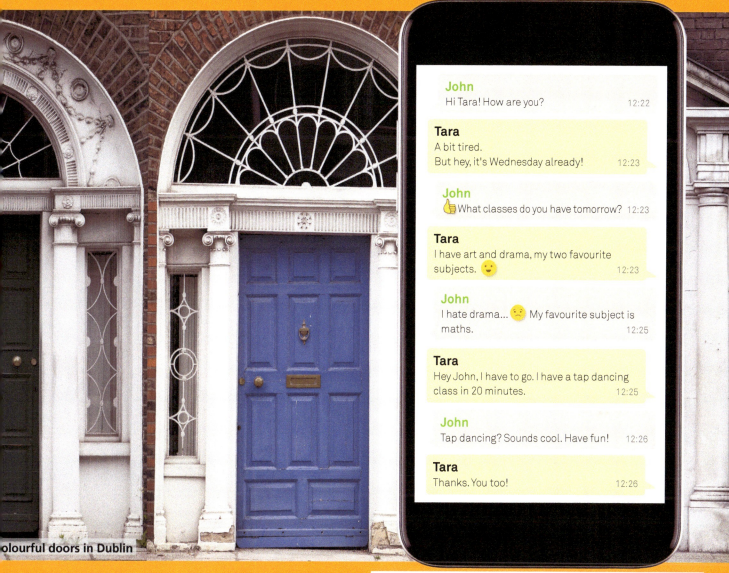

↑ Colourful doors in Dublin

John
Hi Tara! How are you? 12:22

Tara
A bit tired.
But hey, it's Wednesday already! 12:23

John
👍 What classes do you have tomorrow? 12:23

Tara
I have art and drama, my two favourite subjects. 😊 12:23

John
I hate drama... 😟 My favourite subject is maths. 12:25

Tara
Hey John, I have to go. I have a tap dancing class in 20 minutes. 12:25

John
Tap dancing? Sounds cool. Have fun! 12:26

Tara
Thanks. You too! 12:26

↑ Tara's vlog.

LET'S GO!

1. **Read** the conversation.
   Answer these questions:
   a. What subjects does Tara have tomorrow?
   b. Does Tara like drama?
   c. What subject does John like?

2. **Look at** the picture from Tara's video. What does she have for breakfast? What do you have for breakfast?
   Tell a partner.

1. Wake up!

I can talk about my everyday activities.

1 What do you do in the morning?
Tell your classmates.
Include one activity you don't do.

> In the morning, first I get up, then...
> Afterwards, I...
> But I don't...

2 **Watch** part 1 of the video about Tara's day. Then discuss with a partner.
- Is your routine similar or different to Tara's routine?
- How do you feel when you haven't got much time in the morning?

have a shower
do my hair | get up
pack my bag | wake up
wash my face | brush my teeth
make my bed | leave home
check my phone | get dressed
eat / have breakfast

↑ Tara's vlog

Vocabulary
Vocabulary track: 07

first
then
afterwards
finally

The present simple tense

I **make** my bed.
≠ I **don't make** my bed.

She **makes** her bed.
≠ She **doesn't make** her bed.

3 **Put** the activities in the right order.
Identify three activities Tara doesn't mention.

4 **Write** two things that your classmates do and one thing they don't.

> Paul gets dressed first and then...
> Isabelle has a shower first...

LET'S PLAY...

The fortune teller game (pair work)
1. **Make** a paper fortune teller.
2. **Draw** daily activities.
3. Student A **says** a number.
4. Student B **shows** him/her the picture for that number.
5. Student A **says** what activity the picture shows.

44 forty-four

Bloggers 1

5 **Watch** part 2 of the video about Tara's day. Do you think her school week is busy or easy? **Talk** to a partner.

Did you know?
In home economics we learn how to do practical activities like cooking, sewing, etc.

6 Look at Tara's timetable. **Write** the missing lessons.

	MONDAY	TUESDAY	WEDNESDAY	THURSDAY	FRIDAY
08:40-09:20	History	Religious Education	Spanish	b) ...	Maths
09:20-10:00	Business Studies	a) ...	History	Civic, Social & Political Education	Science & Natural Studies
10:00-10:40	Music	Maths	Religious Education	English	English
			BREAK		
11:05-11:45	c) ...	Home Economics	English	Art	Civic, Social & Political Education
11:45-12:25	Science & Natural Studies	Home Economics	English	Art	Geography
12:25-13:00	English	Business Studies	Music	Geography	English
			LUNCH		
13:40-14:20	English	Geography	PE	History	PE
14:20-15:00	Maths	English	Business Studies	Drama	d) ...
15:00-15:40	Maths	Science & Natural Studies		Maths	IT

7 **Compare** your timetable with Tara's. WB p. 41

Tara starts school at..., but we start at...
She has business studies, but we don't.
She doesn't have...

8 What are Tara's favourite subjects? **Guess** her favourite school day. WB p. 40

Vocabulary track: 08

Vocabulary
- art
- drama
- IT (Information Technology)
- PE (Physical Education)

Time expressions
On Mondays Fridays...
At seven o'clock eight thirty...
In the morning the afternoon the evening...

LET'S PLAY...

The timetable game (pair work)
1. **Look at** your timetable.
2. Student A **says** a day and an hour.
3. Student B **guesses** the subject.

On Wednesdays at 10 we have...
Maths!

MINI CHALLENGE: A PERFECT DAY AT SCHOOL

You present a new timetable for your class. WB p. 42

1 List your favourite subjects (at least five).
2 Invent your perfect timetable for a day.
3 Present your timetable.

I start at 10 am. First, I have 2 hours of... Then...

2. I play Gaelic football

I can talk about my hobbies.

1 **Watch** part 2 of Tara's video again.
Read the texts and fill in the gaps.
Look at the logos of the schools clubs in Dublin.
Match each student with the correct club.
Tara doesn't mention 2 logos. WB p. 43

Did you know?
Irish, or Gaelic, is an official language of the Republic of Ireland, in addition to English.

Callum: I love literature and films. On a) ... evenings, I go to a drama club with my brother. We want to be professional actors!

Sophie: I love reading books and writing poems. On b) ..., I always go to a club to learn how to write.

Tara: In my free time, I do c) ... twice a week. I love it! I also like surfing the Net at home.

Aidan: In the d) ..., I usually play e-sports, and once a week, I practise with my Gaelic football team.

2 Do you have anything in common with them?
Talk about what you do in your free time.

In my free time, sometimes I play rugby...
I usually surf the Net, like Tara.

Adverbs of frequency

| always | sometimes |
| usually | never |

LET'S PLAY...

The truth game
1. **Write** three activities you do in your free time: two are true but one is false.
2. **Read** them aloud.
3. The others **guess** the false one.

I play the guitar, I learn Greek and...

False! You don't play the guitar. You play the piano!

Vocabulary — Vocabulary track: 09

to chat with my friends
to cook
to do football/tennis training
to draw
to go to dance/drama classes
to listen to music / the radio...
to play the violin / the guitar...
to play video games
to read a book
to sing
to speak a foreign language
to surf the Internet
to watch films/TV/videos
to write

4 **Imagine** it's your birthday. You have a party with friends and family. Who do you invite from your family? **Tell** a partner. WB p. 26

5 **Watch** Tom's video about his birthday party. Who is at the party? **Draw** the family tree.

↑ Tom's vlog.

Vocabulary track: 05

Vocabulary
husband
wife
uncle
aunt
nephew
niece
cousin

Review: Possessive adjectives

I: my
You: your
He/She: his / her

LET'S PLAY…

She's my grandmother!

He's my grandson!

The game of the family relationships (group work)
1. **Sit down** in a circle.
2. Student A **points at** student B and **invents** a family relationship.
3. Student B **answers** by saying the family relationship for him/her.

MINI CHALLENGE: A FAMILY GAME (group work)

Play the family game: invent a famous family for yourself! WB p. 28

STUDENT A:

1 **Imagine** a family with yourself and six or seven famous characters (real or fictional).
2 **Draw** the family tree.

STUDENT B:

1 **Explain** the family tree to student C.

STUDENT C:

1 **Listen** to student B and **draw** the family tree.

Beyoncé Lionel Messi

me   my sister

His father is Lionel Messi…

2. Have you got blue eyes?

I can describe a person's physical appearance.

 1 Look at this family.
Read the descriptions of the members of the family.
Underline the information about physical characteristics. WB p. 29

Lewis has got one child, Tom. **Tom** is medium height. He has got brown eyes and brown hair.
Jen has got a sister, Lisa. **Jen** is tall and she has got red hair. **Lisa** is tall and she has got blonde hair.
Jess has got two daughters, **Maria** and **Eva**. They are the intelligent girls of the family. They have got long dark hair and brown eyes.

 2 Listen to the description and complete the sentence. WB p. 29

Track: 04

Her name is Maria and she's ... years old. She's ... and she is very .... She has got ... hair and brown ....

 3 Write a description of another character in this family. Your partner guesses who they are! WB p. 29

 LET'S PLAY…

The 'Stand up if…' game
1. A student **says** a sentence with a physical feature.
2. **Stand up** if it applies to you.

Stand up if you've got brown eyes!

Vocabulary (Vocabulary track: 06)

black/dark hair
blond(e) hair
brown hair
red hair

4 **Read** the extract from the famous novel 'Little Women'. **Match** the descriptions with the girls in the image. WB p. 32

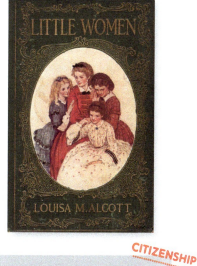

Margaret, the eldest of the four, is sixteen, and very pretty. She has got big eyes, brown hair, a sweet mouth, and white hands.

Fifteen-year-old Jo is very tall and thin. She has
5 got beautiful long brown hair. And she has got big hands and feet.

Elizabeth, or Beth, as everyone calls her, is thirteen. She has got bright eyes, soft hair, a shy manner and a timid voice.

10 Amy, though the youngest, is a most important person, in her own opinion at least. She has got blue eyes and blonde hair.

↑ Louisa May Alcott, **Little Women** (1868)

CITIZENSHIP

Types of family

1. **Describe** your family. Who are they? What do they look like?
The others draw a family picture.
Discuss which drawing you take home to show your family.

 5 **Ask** and **answer** questions about a member of your partner's family. **Exchange** roles.

- Have you got a sister?
◦ Yes, I have.

- Is she tall? Has she got...?
◦ No, she isn't. She's got...

Asking questions with **have got** and
She has got blue eyes.   **She is** tall.
Has she got blue eyes?   **Is she** tall?
✓ Yes, **she has**.   ✓ Yes, **she is**.
✗ No, **she hasn't**.   ✗ No, **she isn't**.

2. **Look at** all the other pictures. Are all families the same? **Explain** the differences ...

Kim has got two brothers, one uncle ...

 MINI CHALLENGE: WHO'S WHO? (pair work)

Play 'Who's Who' and guess your partner's character. WB p. 33

1 **Invent** a character and draw a picture.
Give your character a name.
2 **Hang** all the portraits on the wall.
3 **Ask** questions to identify your partner's character.
4 **Answer** your partner's questions.

Has he got...?

Is he...?

Yes, he has.

My grammar → Exercises p. 115

I understand and I practise.

1. THE VERB HAVE GOT WB p. 25, 32

- The verb **have got** allows you to express:
- ownership (**I have got a computer**),
- family ties (**I have got a brother**),
- physical descriptions (**I have got long hair**).

POSITIVE FORM		
I / You	have got	blue eyes. long hair.
He / She / It	has got	
We / You / They	have got	

- In spoken English, contract **I have got** to **I've got**. The word **have** becomes **'ve**. **He/she has got** becomes **he/she's got**. These are known as "contracted" verbs.

- In the question form, the subject and **have** change position.

QUESTION FORM		
Have	I / you	got a brother?
Has	he / she / it	
Have	we / you / they	

- In short answers, **got** is not used.

POSITIVE ANSWERS (YES)		
Yes,	I / you	have.
	he / she / it	has.
	we / you / they	have.

NEGATIVE ANSWERS (NO)		
No,	I / you	haven't.
	he / she / it	hasn't.
	we / you / they	haven't.

When talking about your age in English, you use **to be** instead of **have got**.
I'm 11 (years old).
Do you know what happens in any other languages?

---

1 Complete the sentences with the correct form of the verb **have got**.

a. ..... you ..... any brothers or sisters?
Yes, I ..... .

b. ..... your sister ..... blue eyes?
Yes, she ..... .

c. ..... your cousins ..... a dog?
No, they ..... .

d. ..... Matt ..... a cousin?
Yes, he ..... .

2 Rewrite the following about Lucy.

Hi! My name is Lucy. I have got a big family. I have got three brothers, Billy, Jim and Scott, and two sisters, Mandy and Carla. I have got a dog and a cat, too. I've got four uncles and five aunts. So I've got 32 cousins!

Her name is Lucy. She...

3 Write the contracted form of the verb **have got**.

a. My aunt has got two brothers. .....
b. I have got a younger sister. .....
c. My grandmother has got three cats. .....
d. My uncle has got two houses. .....

Pronunciation → WB p. 36

The contracted forms of **have got** and **has got**

2. THE PRESENT TENSE OF THE VERB TO BE (2)

- The form of **to be** with he/she = **is**

  He**'s** my brother.
  Mike**'s** my best friend.

POSITIVE FORM		
He / She	is / 's	my brother / my sister.

- In the negative form, add **not** after the verb **is**. In spoken English, **is not** becomes **isn't**.

NEGATIVE FORM		
He / She	is not / isn't	my brother / my sister.

- To ask a question, you should invert the subject and **is**.

QUESTION FORM		
Is	he / she	your brother / your sister?

- In addition to **he** and **she**, there is also **it**. **It** is used to talk about objects, for example:
  It is a bike.
  It isn't a car.

---

4 Read the text. Who are the two boys in photos 1 and 2?

I'm Tom. I've got two best friends: Shawn and Kyle. They are my classmates. Shawn's got two stepbrothers and Kyle's got a sister. Shawn's got dark hair. Kyle's got short blond hair.

Copy out the text again, using the full verb instead of the contracted form of the verb.

---

3. POSSESSIVE ADJECTIVES WB p. 28

- Possessive adjectives allow you to indicate who an object belongs to and describe family relationships.

This is my bike.   **Kev is my cousin.**

I	my
you	your
he	his
she	her

Watch out! In the third-person singular, the possessive adjective depends on if the owner is male (**his** father) or female (**her** father).

5 Fill in the correct possessive adjective.
a. I have got a cousin. ..... name is Joe.
b. My favourite actress is Emma Watson. I love ..... films.
c. ..... family is very small. I haven't got a brother or a sister.
d. Are you American? I like ..... accent.

Translate the phrases below into your language: "my sister", "my uncle", "my grandparents". What do you notice in comparison to English?

4. ADJECTIVE POSITION WB p. 30

- Adjectives are used to describe nouns. In English, adjectives are places before the noun.

an intelligent girl   **an intelligent boy**
   adjective   noun   adjective   noun

Look at the adjectives in the examples above. Do they change depending on the noun? Do they change in your language?

My vocabulary
→ Exercises, p. 115
→ WB p. 34

I see and I memorise.

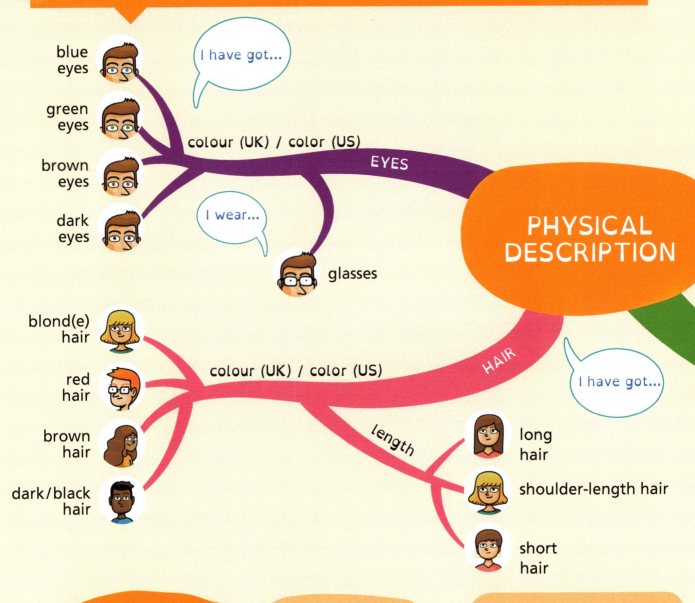

3 **Read** an interview with a young Irish dancer. What do you learn about Jean? WB p. 45

HEALTH EDUCATION

healthy body + healthy mind = happy life

A happy life

1. **Look at** the picture.
   a. **Name** three activities you can do to have a healthy body.
   b. **Name** three activities you can do to have a healthy mind.

A SUCCESSFUL GIRL

From the outside, Jean Kennedy seems like an ordinary girl, but the medals (she placed third in the Irish Dancing World Championship) tell a different story. In this interview, we chat about
5 normal teenage things: friends, college (Jean is studying biology and teaching PE in Dublin City University), family and boyfriends.

I: How often do you practise?
10 J: I go to dance classes every week, but when I prepare for a championship it's much more than that. I spend hours just on one dance.

I: Does performing stop you from
15 doing other things?
J: Yes, it does, a little, but to be honest, I like it that way. My social life is based around my dancing friends, because we're often together
20 and share the same interests.

I: What advice do you have for young dancers?
J: I think young people spend too much time on social networks and the Internet.
25 You should focus on yourself, and build on your character to be a nicer person.

Siún Lennon, **Interview: Jean Kennedy, Irish Dancing World Champion**

Question words

What...?
What time...?
When...?
How...?
How often...?

Questions

Do you...?

✓ Yes, I **do**. / ✗ No, I **don't**.
✓ Yes, he **does**. / ✗ No, he **doesn't**.
✓ Yes, we **do**. / ✗ No, we **don't**.

 MINI CHALLENGE: A CLASS SURVEY (pair work)

You do a class survey to find out if your class is more sporty or more artistic. WB p. 47

1 **Ask** and **answer** questions about sports and art. **Take notes**.

2 **Fill in** a table: the sports/artistic activities that your classmates do, and how often.

3 **Explain** your findings to the class.

4 Is the class more sporty or more artistic?

Do you do any sport?

Yes, I do. I play tennis.

My grammar → Exercises p. 116

I understand and I practise.

1. THE PRESENT SIMPLE WB p. 39

The present simple tense expresses actions happening now and regular actions.

- To make the simple present, use the infinitive verb (without *to*). Remember in the third-person singular add an **-s**.

  I sing in a choir. → She sing**s** in a choir.

- If the verb root ends in **-o, -s, -z, -ch, -sh** or **-x**, then we add **-es**.

  Tara go**es** to tap dance once a week.

- If the verb root ends in **-y** (*study*), then the **y** becomes **i + es**.

  She stud**ies** Irish at school.

Use **do/does** for:
- questions
- negative answers
- short responses

I / you / we / they **do**.
He / she / it **does**.

POSITIVE FORM		
I / You / We	dance	on Mondays.
He / She	dances	

NEGATIVE FORM		
I / You / We	don't	dance on Mondays.
He / She	doesn't	

QUESTION FORM		
Do	I / you / we	dance on Mondays?
Does	he / she	

POSITIVE ANSWERS (YES)		
Yes,	I / you / we	do.
	he / she	does.

NEGATIVE ANSWERS (NO)		
No,	I / you / we	don't.
	he / she	doesn't.

Pronunciation → WB p. 50
"-s" and "-es" in the third-person singular
Sentence stress

- The word order in a sentence depends on the type of sentence:

- In the affirmative:
  She surfs the Net.
  subject + verb + complement

- In the negative:
  She doesn't surf the Net.
  subject + auxiliary + **not** + verb + complement

- In the question form:
  Does she surf the Net?
  auxiliary + subject + verb + complement

- When there is a question word:
  When does she surf the Net?
  question word + auxiliary + subject + verb + complement

In the present simple, the verb only changes form in the third-person singular: **he/she/it**. In question and negative forms, the auxiliary verb changes form: **do/does**.
What happens in your language?

1 Write the verbs in brackets in the present simple tense.

1. You ...... at six o'clock in the morning. (get up)
2. Tara ...... home economics at school. (study)
3. We ...... school at 4:30 pm in France. (finish)
4. You ...... TV in the evening. (watch)
5. Tara ...... Irish dancing. (do)
6. Megan ...... Gaelic football. (play)

2 Rewrite the sentences above in the negative form, then in the question form.

1.
2.
3.
4.
5.
6.

2. TIME EXPRESSIONS WB p. 42

To talk about when an action happens, we use prepositions: **on**, **at** and **in**.

- **on** + day of the week:
  On Wednesdays, I play rugby with my friends.
- **at** + time:
  Tara gets up **at** 7 o'clock.
- **in** + time of day:
  I usually do my homework **in** the evening.

> **3** **Complete** these sentences with the correct prepositions.
>
> At school, Tara has lunch ..... one o'clock. ..... Wednesday, she finishes ..... 3 o'clock ..... the afternoon. She studies French ..... Wednesday and Thursday ..... 8:40 am.

3. ADVERBS OF FREQUENCY WB p. 43

Adverbs of frequency express **how often** something happens. They are placed *before* the verb (except for the verb **to be**, when they are placed *after* the verb).

always   usually   sometimes   never

I **always** chat with my friends.
I **usually** listen to music on my way to school.
I **sometimes** do my homework in the evening.
I **never** watch TV.

> **4** **Place** the adverbs correctly in the following sentences.
>
> (always) On Tuesdays after school, Sean has extra coaching in maths. (usually) After that, he plays the saxophone. (sometimes) In his free time, he surfs the Net. (always) During the week, Sean is with his friend Tom. They get on very well!

4. QUESTION WORDS (2) WB p. 46

Question words are always placed at the start of a question.

| What? |
| What time? |
| When? |
| How often? |
| Where? |

- We use **what time** to provide information about time.
- We use **when** to talk about about the time of day:

What time do you get up in the morning?   At 7 o'clock.

- **When** do you go to the acting club?
  ◦ In the afternoon, on Mondays.
- We use **how often** to talk about the frequency of an activity:
  - **How often** do you play rugby?
  ◦ Never.

> **5** **Write** the questions.
>
> 1. .....? I do my homework every day.
> 2. .....? I finish school at 4:30 pm on Tuesday.
> 3. .....? I go to the cinema on Sunday.
> 4. .....? I have lunch at school on Friday.
> 5. .....? I usually do my homework in my room.

In English, question words contain the letters **wh** (**when**, **what**). Which letters are normally found in question words in your language?

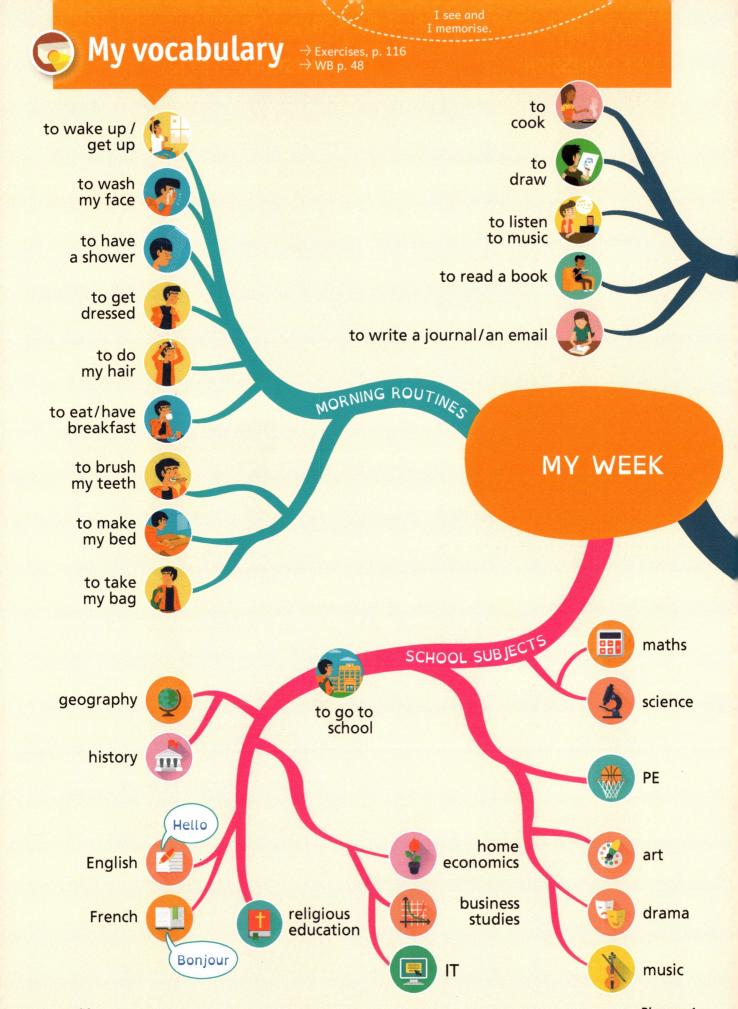

Pronunciation → WB p. 50
How to pronounce "ea"

FREE TIME ACTIVITIES
- to speak a foreign language
- to go to dance classes
- to do football training
- to sing
- to play the violin
- to chat with my friends
- to watch films/TV/videos
- to play video games
- to surf the Internet

SCHOOL SUBJECTS

1 Match the subjects to the photos.

geography   IT   home economics
PE   music   art   maths

 1
 2
 3
 4
 5
 6
 7

HOBBIES AND ACTIVITIES

2 Think about the activities you can do...

a. with a computer: ....
b. in the kitchen: ....
c. with a friend: ....
d. alone: ....
e. with a tablet: ....
f. with a pen: ....
g. with headphones: ....

3 Say three things you **always** do, **sometimes** do and **never** do.

a. always: ....
b. sometimes: ....
c. never: ....

Create your mind map!
Create a mind map by choosing the words that describe your school, subjects, daily activities and hobbies.

Today I'm writing about two very Irish activities. Ireland is a country where traditions are very important.

TWO VERY IRISH ACTIVITIES

↑ Gaelic football

↑ Irish dancing shoes

GAELIC FOOTBALL

Gaelic football is one of the most popular sports in Ireland. This game is played between two teams of 15 players with a round ball.

The aim is to score by kicking or punching the ball into the other team's goals (3 points) or between two posts above the goals (1 point). Girls can play too! Join the #Gaelic4Girls team!

IRISH DANCING

Irish dancing is a Celtic tradition. In Ireland, people like to invite friends to play music, dance and tell stories. Today, Irish boys and girls carry on the tradition of Irish step dancing. In this dance, the feet make quick and precise movements but the arms don't move. You can dance solo or in groups. The costumes are usually very colourful and bright. There are national and international championship competitions.

And I found this really cool video. Watch it to find out more about what's going on in Dublin!

Other Posts:
- Multicultural London: India
- Family Paintings
- Tim Burton's Houses
- London Fashion Design
- I Love Baseball
- New York Skyscrapers
- Scottish Legends

Contributors:

 Sheena

 Tom

 Tara

 John

 Kirstine

YOUR TURN!

1 **Read** the texts. **Look at** the pictures. What's your favourite Irish activity?

YOU ARE AN ARTIST!
Create a logo to represent a new Gaelic football team or an Irish dancing club.

Your challenge

PRESENT YOUR DAY TO YOUR IRISH FRIEND

Tara wants to know about a typical school day in your country.

1. **Think about** what you do on a normal school day.
2. **Find** pictures representing the activities.
3. **Create** a slideshow with pictures to illustrate your day.
4. **Prepare** a short text for each picture.
5. **Present** your day. The class will **choose** the best presentation for Tara.

↓ Digital alternative
Create a video to show what you normally do in your daily routine.

This is a typical school day for me in Portugal. I usually get up at 7… Then I…

WHAT TIME DO YOU GET UP?

To show you have completed this challenge, mark your progress in this unit on the **CHECK YOUR SKILLS** section of your Workbook (p. 51).

Unit 4
Home, sweet home

What are houses and home life like in America?

In this unit, we are going to…
- describe an American house.
- talk about our rooms and housework.
- talk about gender equality.
- discover an American director.

Your challenge

Imagine an unusual house and family for Tim Burton's next film.

Hi, I'm **JOHN**, from Los Angeles, California. In this unit you will learn about American houses.

↑ Residential Neighborhood in Los Angeles, California

↑ John's vlog

LET'S GO!

 Track: 05

1 **Listen to** the Skype conversation.
Complete the sentences.
a. John has a big … in front of his house.
b. His house is very …
c. There are … bedrooms.

2 **Look** at the picture from John's video. What do you think of his bedroom?
Tell a partner.

fifty-five **55**

1. Welcome to my house!

I can describe a house.

1 Look at the ground floor plan of John's house.
Label the rooms you can see.
Then **identify** objects you can see.

> kitchen   living room   garden   toilet
> hall   bathroom   bedroom   study

Did you know?
In the UK, it's ground floor and first floor. In the US, it's first floor and second floor.

Vocabulary — Vocabulary track: 10

- an **a**rmchair
- a b**a**thtub
- a bed
- a chair
- a couch, a s**o**fa
- a chest of dr**a**wers
- a desk
- a f**i**replace
- a lamp
- a m**i**rror
- a **n**ightstand / a b**e**dside t**a**ble
- a T**V**
- a w**a**rdrobe / a closet
- a (wash) b**a**sin / a sink

2 **Watch** John's video. WB p. 52
Discuss John's question at the end with your partner. Can you remember the objects he talks about?
Work with a partner.

> In the kitchen, there are ...

> In the living room, there is a ...

3 **Imagine** you are in John's house.
Describe the room you are in. You partner **guesses** the room.

> You are in ...!

> There is a bed near the window. In front of it ...

there is / there are
There is a bathroom.
There are three bathrooms.

The possessive ('s)
Lisa's room.
The room of Lisa.

4 a. **Look at** John's room. **Listen to** the locations of four objects. **Identify** the objects. WB p. 55

b. John can't find his backpack, his skateboard or his pencil case. **Help** him find them. WB p. 55

The backpack is under the...

Vocabulary
Vocabulary track: 11

- behind
- between
- in front of
- near / next to
- on
- under

The negative form of have got
We **have got** a couch. (UK)
We **haven't got** a garden. (UK)
We **have** a couch. (US)
We **don't have** a garden. (US)

5 In pairs, **ask** and **answer** questions about your own bedroom.

- *How many lamps have you got?*
- *I have got... And you? Have you got posters on the wall?*
- *No, I haven't. I...*

The question form of have got
Have you got a mirror? (UK)
Do you have a mirror? (US)
How many mirrors **have you got**?

LET'S PLAY...

The 'Go fish' game

1. Each player **receives** four cards. On each card, there is a piece of furniture on one side and a room on the other side.
2. The aim is to **collect** furniture to **complete** a room. Player A **asks** player B for a piece of furniture.
3. If player B has the piece of furniture, they **give** the card to player A and player A can **ask** again. If not, player B **says** "Go fish! and player A **takes** another card from the pack.

Marion, have you got a mirror for my bedroom?

No, sorry. Go fish!

I have! Here you are.

MINI CHALLENGE: HOME FOR SALE

This house is for sale. Write the advert. WB p. 56

1 **Draw** the house plan.
2 **Write** a description of the house (rooms, furniture).
3 Don't forget to **include** the price.

Bloggers 1

2. Home rules

I can talk about my room and housework.

 1 **Look at** these people at home.
Describe what they are doing and where they are. WB p. 57

The boys... and... in the...

Vocabulary — Vocabulary track: 12

- to cook
- to do the homework
- to eat my meals
- to go on the computer
- to hang out with friends
- to have a bath
- to have breakfast
- to listen to music
- to read
- to sleep
- to study
- to watch TV

 2 **a. Describe** this room.
  b. Read the poem. What is there in Edwina's favourite room? What does she do there?
  c. Write the first stanza of a poem about your favourite room. WB p. 59

*My favourite place is my desk because
I love drawing...*

My favourite room is where I write.
I spend many hours there.
Morning, mid-day, even at night
in my favourite rocking chair.

5 My piano and my PC friends
I also occupy.
There's just one window in the room
that allows me a view of the sky.

(...)

I would not trade this little room for a
10 castle or a suite.
For the comfort this room gives to me
makes me feel complete.

↑ Edwina Reizer, **My Favorite Room**

 3 Look at the vocabulary list. **Tell** your partner where you usually do the activities.

- *I usually study in my room. What about you?*
- *Sometimes in my bedroom, sometimes...*

4 **Read** the board in John's house. What mustn't he do at home?
Listen to the audio about the chores in John's house.
What do John and Ann have to do this week? WB p. 60

Track: 07

John has to... and he mustn't...

Equality of men and women

1. Why do you think the sculpture is controversial?

2. In your home, who does the laundry? Who cleans the floor? Do you think these are women's jobs or men's jobs?

↑ Chris Madden, **Metaphor for Gender Stereotypes**

5 **Read** these sentences from the video.
Look at the words in purple. Who or what do they refer to?

a. It's my turn to do **them**.
b. Nobody cooks like **me**.
c. I hang out with **him**.
d. It's up to **us**.
e. He always copies **her**.
f. Tonight it's **you**.

Object pronouns

Nobody cooks like **her**.

6 What do you have to do at home? What don't you have to do? Is there anything that you mustn't do? **Tell** a partner.

I have to wash the dishes and I mustn't tell lies...

Obligation and prohibition

I **have to** wash the dishes.
I **must** respect everybody.
I **don't have to** cook.
I **mustn't** tell lies.

MINI CHALLENGE: CRAZY HOME RULES (group work)

Invent crazy house rules. WB p. 61

1 **Imagine** you have a new house and live together.
2 **Write** five chores and activities that you have to / don't have to do.
3 **Present** your rules to the class. Vote for the craziest home.

My grammar → Exercises p. 117

I understand and I practise.

1. THERE IS / THERE ARE WB p. 53

There is / there are indicates something exists.
- **There is** is followed by a singular noun.
  There is a table in the kitchen.
- **There are** is followed by a plural noun.
  There are plates on the table.

> In English, **there is** and **there are** refer to one or several things. Is it the same in your language?

"There is an armchair, and there are four chairs..."

2. THE POSSESSIVE WB p. 54

- The possessive form expresses possession. The name of the person is followed by 's and then the object.

  John's house
  belongs to John

  "The house of John" makes an assumption the student's first language is structured this way.

- When the names are plural or end in an **s**, add an apostrophe to show possession.

  My parent**s'** bedroom is very big.
  My cousin**s'** house has got a swimming pool.

Pronunciation → WB p. 64
The pronunciation of "'s"
There is / there are and there isn't / there aren't

1 Place **'s** in the correct place in the sentences below.
a. John bedroom is really cool.
b. I don't like John couch.
c. Emily loves John garden.
d. I love Andy room.

3. THE NEGATIVE FORM OF HAVE GOT

Haven't got is the negative form of **have got**. It allows you to talk about something that the subject does <u>not</u> have.

I **haven't got** a big house.
He **hasn't got** a garage.

NEGATIVE FORM		
I / You	haven't got	
He / She	hasn't got	a playroom.
We / You / They	haven't got	

> British and American people both speak English, but with some small differences. For example, Americans generally do not use **got**, and instead make the negative form of **have** with the auxiliary verb **do/does**:
>
> I **don't have** a big house.
> He **doesn't have** a garage.

2 Write these sentences in the negative.
a. Emily has a big room.
b. Emily's family has a nice house.
c. My aunt has a fireplace in her house.
d. John has two brothers and two sisters.
e. John has a computer in his room.
f. John's parents have a nice bedroom.

4. HOW MANY?

How many is used to ask about quantity. It is at the beginning of a question. It is always followed by a plural.

We can use it as follows:
- **Have got**:
  How many brothers and sisters **have** you **got**?
- **There is** / **there are**:
  How many bathrooms **are there** in your house?
- With other verbs:
  How many people **do** you usually **invite** to your parties?

> **3** Use the words to make questions.
> a. how / bathrooms / you / got ?
> b. many / hours / you / normally / sleep?
> c. many / rooms / there / your house?
> d. how / computers / are / your house?

5. OBJECT PRONOUNS WB p. 60

Object pronouns are used to replace nouns.

He loves Jane. → He loves **her**.
I like fireplaces. → I like **them**.

SINGULAR		PLURAL	
I	→ me	we	→ us
you	→ you	you	→ you
he	→ him	they	→ them
she	→ her		
it	→ it		

> **4** Complete the sentences below.
> a. Who is this boy? Do you know ..... ?
> b. She wants to invite Lola, Paul and Adam. She likes ..... a lot.
> c. Mum is a great chef. Nobody cooks like ..... .
> d. I don't like this city. I hate ..... .

6. OBLIGATION AND PROHIBITION WB p. 61

Obligation can be expressed using **must** or **have to**. Both options are placed before the verb.

I **have to** work.
You **must** buy him a present.

Make the negative form by adding **not to** (**n't**).
- **Mustn't** shows something that is prohibited.
  You **mustn't** tell lies.
- **Don't have to** shows something that is not obligatory.
  You **don't have to** come.

You **have to** wash the dishes before going out!

> **5** Complete the sentences with must or mustn't.
> a. You ..... arrive late. They are waiting for you!
> b. You ..... listen to your teacher, John.
> c. I ..... eat French fries and hamburgers every day or I'll get fat.
> d. Your children ..... jump on the bed!
> e. I haven't got a lot of money. I ..... waste it.

> **6** Choose the correct form for the sentences below.
> a. Are you quiet in class? You **have to**/**don't have to** be quiet in class.
> b. Do you wear uniforms in France? You **have to**/**don't have to** wear uniforms in France.
> c. Do you have to turn off your phones in theatres? You **have to**/**don't have to** turn off your phones in theatres.
> d. Do you have to bring food to school in your country? You **have to**/**don't have to** bring food to school in your country.

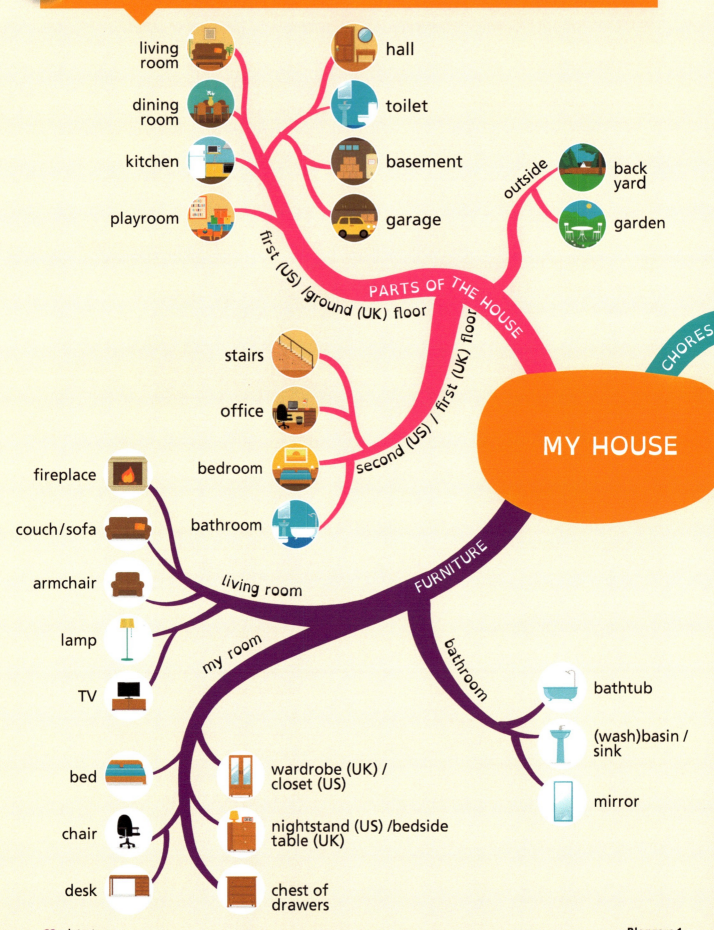

ROOMS IN A HOUSE

1 **Name** each room in a house.

FURNITURE

2 **Say** which piece of furniture, room or object in the picture above corresponds to each description.
a. It's under the bathroom mirror.
b. It's next to the couch.
c. It's in front of the desk.
d. It's next to the bathroom sink.
e. It's in front of the couch.
f. It's between the two bedside tables.

CHORES AND ACTIVITIES IN THE HOME

3 **Identify** the activities below.
a. Sometimes I .... for my family. They love my spaghetti carbonara.
b. I always .... in my room. I have a big desk.
c. My sister always .... . She loves animals.
d. I always .... the table before dinner.
e. I like to recycle. I always .... in the evening.
f. All my clothes are dirty! I must ....
g. I .... my bedroom every day. I hate it when my room is dirty.

Create your mind map!
Create a mind map by choosing the words that correspond to your house, what you do there, and the chores you have to do...

Today I'm writing about two famous fictional houses by Tim Burton.

ARTISTIC AND CULTURAL EDUCATION

TIM BURTON'S HOUSES

TIM BURTON

I love cinema, and Tim Burton is one of my favorite filmmakers! In his films, the houses are always interesting.

In **Charlie and the Chocolate Factory**, the house is poor and dark, but inside it's warm and inviting. There is a strong connection with Charlie's character. The house is different from the rest of the city, just like Charlie is different from the other kids.

↑ This style of house reflects Charlie's poor family on the outside

↑ Tim Burton's **Alice in Wonderland** is full of magic. This castle shows the magic Alice experiences.

↑ In the film **Edward Scissorhands**, Edward lives on a street similar to this one. The houses are identical, but they each have a personality.

YOUR TURN!

1 **Read** the texts and **identify** the adjectives used to describe the houses.

2 **Match** these adjectives to one of the images. **Explain** your choices.

| new | colourful | peculiar | conventional | lonely | spacious | small |

YOU ARE AN ARTIST!

Invent your own house that fits your personality. **Draw** it.

Other Posts:
- Multicultural London: India
- Family Paintings
- Two Very Irish Activities
- London Fashion Design
- I Love Baseball
- New York Skyscrapers
- Scottish Legends

Contributors:

 Sheena

 Tom

 Tara

 John

 Kirstine

Your challenge

DESIGN AN UNUSUAL HOUSE

Tim Burton is looking for ideas for unusual houses and characters for a new film. You decide to send him some ideas.

1. Your teacher will give you a template of a house.
2. **Name** the different rooms and pieces of furniture. Remember it has to be a bit strange!
3. **Imagine** the members of the family who live in the house. **Give** them names.
4. **Write** what each member does in each room (favourite activity or household chores).
5. **Think of** unusual house rules.
6. **Present** your house and your family to the class.
7. **Record** each presentation and send the best one to Tim!

↓ Digital alternative
Make a video that shows your house and explains what you and your family members do in each room.

"This is the skateboard house. On the first floor, there is a living room and..."

Mike

"Gloria, the mother, usually reads on the sofa and Mike, the father, feeds the cat on his skateboard every day. I..."

To show you have completed this challenge, mark your progress in this unit on the **CHECK YOUR SKILLS** section of your Workbook (p. 65).

Unit 5
Looking good!

How do London teenagers dress and where do they shop?

→ **In this unit we are going to...**
- talk about dress codes.
- learn how to communicate in a shop.
- discover a famous London stylist.
- give our opinion on wearing school uniforms.

Your challenge

Design and present a new collection of school uniforms for Marks & Spencer.

Hi, this is **SHEENA**, from London (UK). In this unit you'll learn about clothes and shopping in London.

↑ Oxford Street, London

John
Hi Sheena! Where are you? What are you doing? 11:48

Sheena
Hi! I'm in Oxford Street. I'm looking for a new pair of trainers. What about you? 11:49

John
I'm at home, studying. 11:49

Sheena
Hey, do you like these (the pink ones)? 11:50

John
Yes! They're cool. 11:50

↑ Sheena's vlog

LET'S GO!

1 **Read** the conversation. What are Sheena and John doing? **Complete** the sentences.
 a. Sheena is…
 b. John is…

2 **Look** at the picture from Sheena's video. What do you think it's about? **Tell** a partner.

sixty-seven **67**

1. What are you wearing?

I can talk about outfits.

1 **Identify** the different items of clothing in the photos. WB p. 66
Watch part 1 of Sheena's video.
Draw lines to match the school uniform that boys and girls must wear.
Why do you think boys and girls have a different uniform?
Discuss in a group.

ST. SWITHIN'S HIGH SCHOOL

Uniform
All students are encouraged to be proud of their appearance and their uniform.

School uniform
- Green blazer with school badge
- Green and white tie
- White shirt
- Grey jumper (optional)
- Grey or white socks
- Grey leather shoes
- Grey skirt and black tights
- School trousers (classic style)

- caps
- hoodies
- trainers
- boots
- jeans
- piercings
- jewellery

2 **Look at** Sheena's clothes.
Say if she can wear these items of clothing at school or not. WB p. 66

Track: 08

At school, she can wear... but she can't wear...

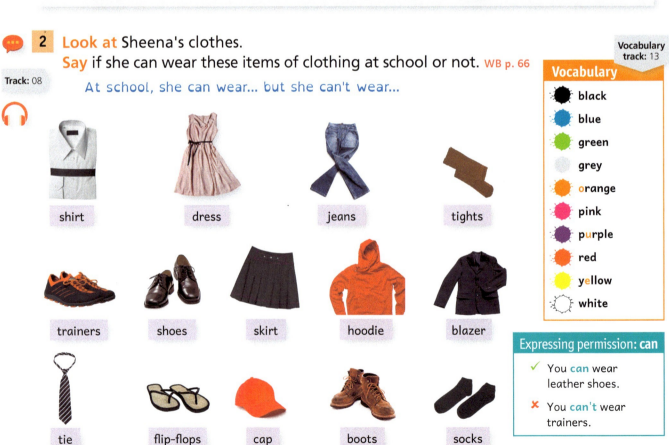

shirt — dress — jeans — tights
trainers — shoes — skirt — hoodie — blazer
tie — flip-flops — cap — boots — socks

Vocabulary track: 13

Vocabulary
- black
- blue
- green
- grey
- orange
- pink
- purple
- red
- yellow
- white

Expressing permission: can
✓ You **can** wear leather shoes.
✗ You **can't** wear trainers.

3 **Watch** part 2 of Sheena's video.
Write the names of the people she interviews under each photo.
Read Sheena's article about fashion in the 'London Teens' mag.
Match the texts and the images. WB p. 69

Ada is wearing...

LONDON TEENS

A They are sixteen and they live in Notting Hill. They are wearing casual clothes: jeans, shirts and hoodies. Jack is wearing a cap too. Here, they are walking around their neighbourhood.

3) ...

B She is fourteen. She lives in Hackney, in the East End. She is wearing a checked jacket and a black shirt and a grey wollen hat. Here, she's taking a picture.

2) ...

C She is fifteen. She lives in Greenwich. Here, she is on her bike. She's wearing a summer look: jeans and a long-sleeved T-shirt with black and white stripes.

1) ...

CITIZENSHIP

School uniforms

Do you think school uniforms are a good or a bad idea? Why/ Why not? You can **use** these words to give your opinion.

beautiful	smart
ugly	original	the same
a symbol of equality	fair
elegant	expensive

↑ Charles Beyl, **CartoonStock**

Vocabulary — Vocabulary track: 14

- spring
- autumn
- summer
- winter

LET'S PLAY... The outfit game
1. **Describe** what a classmate is wearing.
2. Your partner **guess** who it is.

He is wearing blue jeans, white trainers...

It's Mathieu!

The present continuous

I **am** wear**ing** a white cap.
He / She **is** wear**ing** a white cap.

MINI CHALLENGE: TEENS TODAY

'Teen Vogue' wants you to write an article about teen fashion in your country WB p. 71

1 **Find and print** photographs to illustrate the article called 'Local Teens Today'.
2 **Write** a caption for each describing what teens are wearing.
3 **Add** a paragraph to **explain** what students can or can't wear at school.
4 The class will **decide on** the best article to send to 'Teen Vogue'.

2. A shopping day

I learn how to express myself in a shop.

1 **Look at** this map from Sheena's video of a famous shopping street in London. **Identify** all the types of shops on the map. WB p. 72

↑ Josh Hurley, **Camden High Street**

2 **Read** these sentences about Zoe, from Sheena's video.
Explain what the best presents for her birthday are.
Write how much each item costs.
Vote for the best present Sheena can buy. WB p. 73

Zoe

→ Zoe loves hats. She doesn't wear any jewellery. She likes winter sports.

→ She has got two baseball caps, but she hasn't got a beanie. She hasn't got a scarf.

→ Her favourite colours are red and purple, and she hates yellow.

Vocabulary
Vocabulary track: 15

an antique shop
a bookshop / bookstore
a clothes shop
a department store
a gift shop
a market
a shopping centre (UK) = a mall (US)
a sporting goods shop
a toy shop

How much?

How much is this?
It's £15.

How much are these?
They're £12.

flip-flops £   gloves £   rucksack £
bracelet £   scarf £
beanie £   earrings £   baseball cap £

3 It's time to listen to Sheena's final task at London Teens Mag. Sheena and Tessa are looking for a present for their friend Zoe in Camden High Street. **Listen to** the conversation with the shop assistant. What do they finally buy? WB p. 75

Track: 09

Did you know?
In the United Kingdom, the official currency is the pound sterling (£).
one pound = 100 pence
1 pence is a penny.

↑ John Kellerman, **Camden High Street, London**

Vocabulary
Vocabulary track: 16

Can I help you?
I'm l**oo**king for a b**ea**nie / hat…
I love these shoes!
Do you have it in red / blue…?
Here you are.

Agreeing and disagreeing

These shoes are cool.
I **agree**. They're nice!

These shoes are horrible.
I **disagree**. / I **don't agree**.
I like them.

LET'S PLAY…

The Hangman game (pair work)
1. **Think about** a piece of clothing, an accessory or a type of shop.
2. **Tell** your partner the category that you have chosen.
3. Your partner **says** a letter of the alphabet. If your word doesn't contain that letter, then **draw** one part of the hangman.

MINI CHALLENGE: SHOPPING IN LONDON (group work)

Role play a shopping situation in London. WB p. 77

1 STUDENT A: You work as a shop assistant in London.
Use the cards that your teacher gives you.
For each product, **write** the available colours and the price on the back. **Place** the cards on your table.

2 STUDENTS B & C: You are in a shop in London.
You **want** a gift for one of your classmates.
You don't want to **spend** more than £30.

Can I help you?

We are looking for…
I think that she hasn't got…

Bloggers 1

My grammar ⇢ Exercises p. 118

I understand and I practise.

1. EXPRESSING PERMISSION WITH CAN
WB p. 68

- The auxiliary verb **can** expresses possibility.
  You **can** wear jeans.
- The negative form of the verb, **can't** (**cannot**), expresses something that is not possible.
  You **can't** wear trainers.
- **Can** never changes form. It is followed by the verb root.

POSITIVE FORM		
I/You He/She We/They	can/can't	wear trainers.

QUESTION FORM		
Can	I/you/he/she we/they	wear trainers?

POSITIVE ANSWERS (YES)		
Yes,	I/you/he/she we/they	can.

NEGATIVE ANSWERS (NO)		
No,	I/you/he/she we/they	can't.

1 Write these sentences in the negative form.
a. You can wear jeans.
b. We can wear trainers.
c. Yes, she can wear a cap.

2 Write if you can/can't wear these items to a party.

Pronunciation ⇢ WB p. 80
The sound /ə/

2. THE PRESENT CONTINUOUS WB p. 71

The present continuous gives information about what is happening in the present / now.
  Oh, she **is wearing** blue trousers!

- To make the present form of **to be** + verb-**ing**, change the auxiliary verb **to be** but not the main verb, which only takes **-ing** at the end.
- The structure is: **am** / **is** / **are** + verb + ing

POSITIVE FORM		
I	am wearing	
He/She	is wearing	a T-shirt.
You/We/They	are wearing	

NEGATIVE FORM		
I	am not wearing	
He/She	is not wearing	a T-shirt.
You/We/They	are not wearing	

QUESTION FORM		
Am	I	
Is	he/she	wearing a T-shirt?
Are	you/we/they	

- In short answers, we do not repeat the **-ing** form of the verb.

POSITIVE ANSWERS (YES)		
	I	am.
Yes,	he/she	is.
	you/we/they	are.

NEGATIVE ANSWERS (NO)		
	I	am not ('m not).
No,	he/she	is not (isn't).
	you/we/they	are not (aren't).

- What are you wearing now?

I'm wearing a pair of jeans and a T-shirt.

Are you wearing jeans?
Yes, I am. / No, I'm not.

3 Complete the sentences below with to be + verb-ing.
a. I ..... for a new dress. (look)
b. She ..... a new pair of shoes. (wear)
c. What film ..... they .....? (watch)
d. Now I ..... my homework. (do)

4 Write the correct questions and answers.
a. - you / look / for a new pair of trainers? .....
   - Yes .....
b. - What / your classmate / wear? .....
   - .....
c. - What / you / wear / today? .....
   - I .....

5 Choose the present simple or the present form of the verb in brackets.
a. Look! Joe ..... a blue scarf. (wear)
b. She usually ..... a uniform at school. (wear)
c. But today is Sunday and she ..... jeans. (wear)
d. Joe is at the clothes shop. She ..... for a pair of trainers. (look)

3. HOW MUCH? WB p. 74

To ask how much something costs, use **how much** with the verb **to be** or with the verb **cost**.
How much is this bracelet?
How much does this bracelet cost?
It is £16.50. / It costs £16.50.

How much are these gloves?
How much do these gloves cost?
They are £25. / They cost £25.

6 Ask a friend for the price of these items of clothing. Write down the answers in full. Use letters not numbers.

T-shirt ?   trainers ?   skirt ?   shoes ?

4. AGREEING AND DISAGREEING WB p. 76

- Those shoes are really beautiful.
- I agree (with you)! I love the colour!

- Two forms of the negative:
- I disagree (with you)! I don't like the colour.
- I don't agree (with you)! I don't like the style.

7 Respond to these statements.
a. This suit is too big. ✗
b. These trainers are awful. ✓
c. I think the red scarf is perfect for her. ✗
d. This T-shirt is really funny. ✓

Watch out! In English, when we want to express agreement, we do not use the verb **to be** (I am agree), but the verb **agree** by itself (I agree).

8 Write a conversation between two friends visiting Camden Town in London. They want to buy a birthday present for a friend and they do not agree.

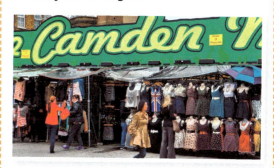

Bloggers 1

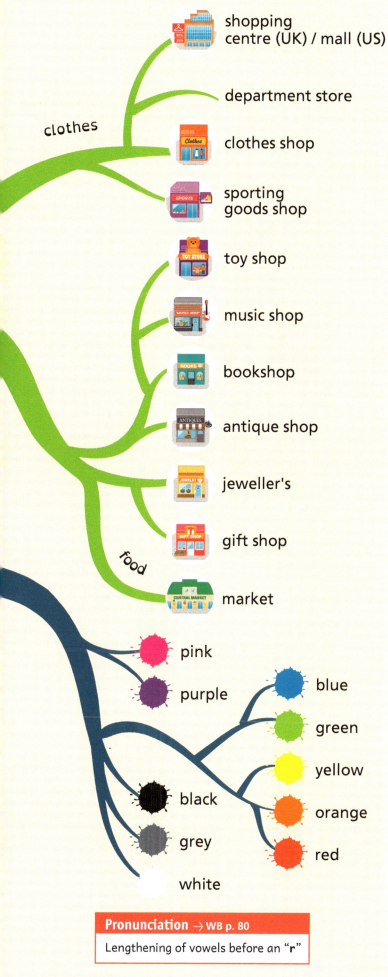

CLOTHES AND COLOURS

1 The stylist at Bigstore has taken notes for the new winter collection.
Design the clothes described by the stylist.

a. pink dress + pink and blue tights

b. red dress with white and yellow stripes

c. orange skirt + blue and orange jumper

d. grey jeans + green t-shirt with "Good morning!" on it

ACCESSORIES

2 **Place** these accessories in the correct column(s).

flip-flops   cap   beanie   scarf   gloves   sunglasses

SUMMER	WINTER

COLOURS

3 **Write** the missing colour.

a. + 🟠 = ...

b. ⚪ + ... = 🩷

c. 🔴 + ... = 🟠

d. ⚫ + ⚪ = ...

e. 🟡 + ... = 🟢

f. + 🔵 = ...

SHOPS

4 In which shop can you find these items?

a. earrings   b. a comic

c. headphones   d. trainers

5 **Give** the answers to these sums in words.

a. 13 + 45 = ...
b. 8 + 28 = ...
c. 99 + 1 = ...
d. 76 + 15 = ...

Create your mind map!
Create your own mind map with your favourite shops, colours, clothes and accessories.

Pronunciation → WB p. 80
Lengthening of vowels before an "r"

Today I'm writing about London teens and fashion.
Do you want to find out about a popular designer from London?

ARTISTIC AND CULTURAL EDUCATION

LONDON FASHION DESIGN

I love design and fashion, and in London there are fantastic designers.

Look at this suit for this summer: red, orange and blue with an African print. I think it's fun and elegant. And the white shirt is very cool too.

How much is it? Very expensive, certainly!

STELLA MCCARTNEY

The outfits are created by a London fashion designer called Stella McCartney. She is very famous in London, and internationally. Her father is famous too. He's Paul McCartney, one of The Beatles. I'm sure you know The Beatles!

She has an original style. Her clothes are often casual and relaxed, and she creates sports outfits too. She wants to protect animals, so she doesn't use animal products (fur or leather) in her creations.

YOUR TURN!

1 **Read** the text and **look at** the models. **Close** your books.
   a. What's the name of the designer Sheena talks about?
   b. What does she want to protect?
   c. Use your memory to describe one of the outfits on the page.

YOU ARE AN ARTIST!

You are Stella McCartney's new assistant designer. **Design** two pieces of clothing that fit with her style and **write** a short paragraph to present them.

Other Posts:
o Multicultural London: India
o Family Paintings
o Two Very Irish Activities
o Tim Burton's Houses
o I Love Baseball
o New York Skyscrapers
o Scottish Legends

Contributors:

 Sheena

 Tom

 Tara

 John

 Kirstine

Your challenge

NEW SCHOOL UNIFORM

M&S EST. 1884

Marks & Spencer's wants you to create a new school uniform.

1. **Decide** if boys and girls wear the same or different uniforms.
2. **Draw** the winter school outfit you want (boys' and girls') in groups of four.
3. **Think about** the accessories, the price, the colours.
4. **Decide** what English students can / can't wear in summer with your outfit.
5. **Present** your collection to the rest of the class.
6. The class **chooses** the best outfit to sell at Marks & Spencer's.

↓ **Digital alternative**
You can scan in your designs and project them, so that they look more professional.

> This is the new uniform. As you can see, this girl is wearing... In summer, students can also wear... but they can't wear...

> Wow! How much are these shoes?

> I don't like this shirt in blue. Do you have it in red?

> I don't agree! I love this colour.

To show you have completed this challenge, mark your progress in this unit on the **CHECK YOUR SKILLS** section of your Workbook (p. 81).

Unit 6
Let's play ball!

> Do they play the same sports in the United States as we do?

▸ **In this unit, we are going to...**
- look at typical American sports.
- talk about sporting talents and a sports diet.
- discuss American enthusiasm for baseball.
- talk about the values of "fair-play".

Your challenge
Create a poster to promote a new American sport.

Hi, this is **JOHN**, from Los Angeles, California. In this unit you'll learn about American sports.

↑ John's vlog

LET'S GO!

1 **Look at** the photograph. What sport can you play in this stadium?

2 **Look** at the video still. What sports can you see? **List** the sports you know. **Compare** with a partner.

1. You mustn't kick the ball!

I can talk about typical American sports.

1 **Look at** the poster backgrounds.
What sports can you see?
What equipment do you need to play these sports? WB p. 82

To play American football, you need...

Did you know?
In the USA there is an intense rivalry between some teams on the east and west coasts.

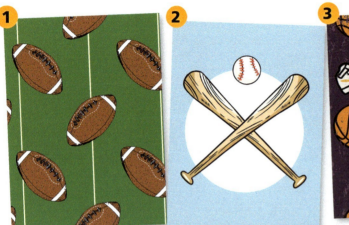

Vocabulary
Vocabulary track: 17

- a (foot / basket / base)ball
- a bat
- a cap
- a facemask
- a glove
- a helmet
- a jersey
- a net
- a racket
- shorts
- shoulder pads
- a stick
- trainers (UK) / sneakers (US)

How can I memorise things? Go to p. 133 to find out!

2 **Watch** part 1 of John's video.
Memorise the rules of baseball.
Close your book and **write** or **draw** the rules in your notebook.
Compare with a partner. WB p. 83

↑ John's vlog: how to play ...

Vocabulary
Vocabulary track: 18

- to bounce = to dribble
- to catch
- to hit
- to jump
- to kick
- to pass
- to push
- to run
- to score
- to shoot
- to sweep = to brush
- to throw

3 **Write** some basic rules of baseball. WB p. 84

To play baseball, you need two teams of...
Players must...

need / need to and must / mustn't

To play basketball you **need** a sleeveless shirt, shorts and sneakers.

You **need to** be fast.

You **must** throw the ball but you **mustn't** kick it.

4 **Watch** part 2 of John's video and **make** notes about ice hockey:
- Equipment and clothes
- Number of players on a team
- The name of the player in goal
- How to win

Did you know?
Americans love competing with Canadians in winter sports, especially ice hockey!

5 **Match** these the sentence halves to complete the rules of ice hockey.
Write similar sentences about the sport of your choice. WB p. 86

To play..., you need...
Players must... but they mustn't...

ICE HOCKEY RULES

1. To play ice hockey, you need a puck:
2. Each player needs a hockey stick
3. To score a goal, players
4. When you commit a foul
5. You must wear protective equipment

a. for your safety, like a helmet and gloves.
b. a small black disk, made of rubber.
c. must shoot the puck into their opponent's net.
d. you must go to the penalty box for 2 minutes.
e. to control, pass and shoot the puck.

6 **Complete** the table. **Compare** your answers with a partner.
Explain your answers.

	Baseball	Hockey
I think John prefers ...		
I prefer ...		

Vocabulary — Vocabulary track: 19

American football
baseball
basketball
boxing
curling
(ice / field) hockey
lacrosse
soccer
tennis

7 Time to find out the sport John chooses!
Read the clues and **guess** the sport.

– You sometimes need gloves.
– You don't need a helmet.
– You mustn't wear ice skates

MINI CHALLENGE: A NEW SPORT

The NCAA (National Collegiate Athletic Association) has launched a worldwide competition to create a new American sport. WB p. 87

1 **Invent** a new sport (a combination of different American sports).
2 **Ask yourself** questions like: Is it a team sport or individual? Do you play it indoors or outdoors?
3 **Give** it a name.
4 **Write down** the rules and the equipment you need.
5 **Present** it to the class in 30 seconds max!

My sport is called...
You need two teams of...
Players must... but...

Bloggers 1 eighty-one 81

2. Becoming a champ

I can talk about sporting talent and diets for athletes.

1 **Read** and **take** the quiz.
What American sport is more appropriate for you? WB p. 88
Quiz your partner. **Report** to the class.

> Léa likes team sports.
> She is active and... She can...

WHICH SPORT IS FOR YOU?

1. What sports do you like to play?
- ● individual sports
- ✤◆▲ team sports
- ▲ indoor sports
- ✤◆ outdoor sports
- ✖ none!

2. What are you like? Circle what best describes you.
- ▲ very active ● quite active ✖ lazy
- ✤◆ very fast ▲ fast ● slow ✖ I hate running
- ▲ tall ● medium-height ● small
- ✤ very strong ✤▲ strong ● weak
- ✤◆▲ skilful ● a bit clumsy ✖ very clumsy

3. Do you like sports that require strategy and thinking?
- ✤▲◆ Yes, I do!
- ●✖ No, I don't.

....

If most of your answers are...

✤ **You are fast and skilful.**
You really can throw, hit and catch a ball. Baseball is the best sport for you!

▲ **You are agile and active.**
You can run up and down the court. You are skilful, so shooting the ball into the basket is not a problem for you. Basketball is your sport.

◆ **You are tough and fast.**
You are not afraid of contact. American football is for you!

● **You are quite fit and active** but baseball, basketball and American football are not for you. There are so many other sports. Find one that corresponds to your personality and your abilities.

✖ **You are not active and competitive at all.**
I guess you have other talents. Maybe you can draw, play an instrument... Find your way!

Vocabulary
Vocabulary track: 20

athletic
active ≠ lazy
competitive
fast ≠ slow
fit ≠ unfit
healthy
skilful ≠ clumsy
strong ≠ weak
tough

can + degrees of ability

I **can** throw a ball **very well**.
I **can** throw a ball **quite well**.
I **cannot** (**can't**) throw a ball **at all**.

Qualifying adverbs

I am **very** fit.
I am **quite** fit.
I am **a bit** unfit.
I am **not** fit **at all**.

2 **Look at** the photo. What can you see?
Read. What do the speakers recommend? WB p. 91

Erik: Hi everyone, I'm Erik Spoelstra of the Miami Heat basketball team and a member of the NBA Fit Team. I'm here with two top basketball players to find out why eating healthy food can help you perform like a champion.

Dwain: Well, I eat fruit and vegetables every day because it gives me the energy I need to play really well and move better than the other players.

Erik: Thanks, Dwain. What about you, Ray?

Ray: Water is a really important part of my pre-game routine. I need it to stay focused and refreshed. Seriously, eating the right food can make you a better athlete. You can't eat junk food and play sports well.

Fair play

1. Identify the values that are fundamental in fair play.

loyalty	tolerance	cheating
honesty	disrespect	sadness
solidarity	injustice	violence

2. What values do you see in the photo?

3. Write a slogan to promote fair play in American sports.

3 **Match** these foods with the categories from the vocabulary box. WB p. 92

Track: 10

 chicken
 pears
 tuna
 water
 tomatoes
 milk
 oranges

 cheese
 rice
 green beans
 eggs
 potatoes
 lettuce
 pasta

Vocabulary
Vocabulary track: 21

d**ai**ry
drinks
fruit
grains
proteins
vegetables

4 **Write** sentences to explain what you need to eat or drink in your opinion to be a champion. WB p. 93

To be a champion, you need to eat... because...

LINKING WORDS

You **need to** eat fruit **and** vegetables, **but** you **mustn't** eat junk food **because** it isn't healthy.

MINI CHALLENGE: A SPORTS CLUB ADVERT

Your favourite sports club wants you to create an advert to promote it. WB p. 93

1 **Choose** a sport you like. What qualities are important for this sport?
2 **Associate** one of these qualities with an animal.
3 **Think of** what you need to eat or drink to perform well in this sport.
4 **Write** three or four sentences to promote your sport. **Follow** the example.
5 **Design** the advert.

Are you fast?
Can you swim like a fish?
To be a swimming champion you need to eat dairy foods.
Join the swimming club!

My grammar → Exercises p. 119

I understand and I practise.

1. NEED / NEED TO MUST / MUSTN'T WB p. 84

To say that we need something, use:

need + noun (or nominal group)

To play American football you need a helmet and protective gear.

need + to + verb

To become a champion, you need to eat healthy food.

To express obligation, use **must**:
To play sports, you must wear trainers.

To express prohibition, use **mustn't**:
You mustn't kick other players.

---

1 Answer one of the questions below.
a. What do you need to play baseball?
b. What do you need to play basketball?

2 Use the prompts to write sentences with need.
a. American football / helmet / protect your head
b. basketball / be fit and agile
c. eat a lot of fruit and vegetables / be fit

3 Choose one sport and describe what you need to / play it.

....
....
....

4 Complete the sentences below with must or mustn't.
a. You .... respect all players in a game.
b. To be a sports champion, you .... eat junk food.
c. In American football protective gear is essential. You .... wear a helmet, a facemask and shoulder pads.
d. In American football, you .... run with the ball, you .... dribble it.

---

2. CAN / CAN'T WB p. 89

- The auxiliary verb **can** expresses possibility or ability.
- The negative form of the verb, **can't** (**cannot**), expresses something that is not possible or a lack of ability (something we are not able to do).
- **Can** and **can't** do not change. They are followed by the verb.
  I can run fast.
  I can't jump high.

POSITIVE FORM		
I / You		
He / She	can	swim.
We / They		

NEGATIVE FORM		
I / You		
He / She	can't (cannot)	swim.
We / They		

In the question form of the verb, invert the verb **can** and the subject.

QUESTION FORM		
	I / you	
Can	he / she	handle a ball?
	we / they	

SHORT ANSWERS		
Yes,	I / you / he / she / we / they	can.
No,		can't.

What is the corresponding word for **can** in your language? Does it change form or not?

Pronunciation → WB p. 96

How to pronounce **can** and **can't**

3. LEVEL OF ABILITY WB p. 90

To express level of ability, use...

- in affirmative sentences:

  can + verb + very/really/quite well

  I can play basketball very / really / quite well.

- in negative sentences:

  can't + verb + at all

  I can't play basketball at all.

> **5** Write sentences about people's abilities. Specify the level of ability.
>
> a. Peter / cycle 👍👍👍👍
> b. Emma / swim 👍👍
> c. Liz and Alison / play badminton 👎👎👎
> d. you / play football 👍👍
>
> **6** Place the words in the right order to ask questions. Then, answer them. Pay attention to punctuation.
>
> a. play / you / curling / can ?
> b. throw / can / a / you / football ?
> c. mother / fast / your / run / can ?
> d. short / basketball / players / can / people / great / be ?

4. ADVERBS OF DEGREE WB p. 90

- An adverb modifies the meaning of a verb or an adjective.
- Some adverbs modify the level or degree of the situation: a little, a lot, very much.

+

↑ I am very / really agile.
  I am quite agile.
  I am a bit slow / lazy.*
  I am not agile at all.

−

* A bit is normally used with negative adjectives.

- They are placed before the adjective they qualify, except at all, which is used in negative phrases and is placed at the end of a sentence.

> **7** Write sentences using the adjectives below to describe yourself. Include adverbs.
>
> athletic healthy
> active   fit
> skilful   lazy
> strong   competitive

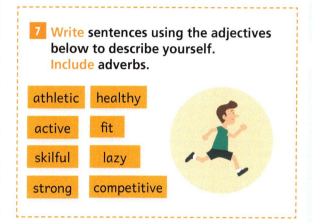

5. LINKING WORDS WB p. 93

A linking word connects two parts of a sentence. It can add information, contrast two ideas or give a reason.

- To add information: and

  You need to eat a lot of fruit and vegetables.

- To contrast two parts of a sentence: but

  You can eat a little butter but you can't eat a lot of chips.

- To give an explanation: because

  Apples are healthy because they contain a lot of vitamins.

> **8** Link the two statements with the correct conjunction.
>
> a. You can eat a lot of lettuce, carrots ... tomatoes.
> b. Rice and pasta are necessary ... they are full of fibre.
> c. You can't eat a lot of biscuits ... you can eat a few.

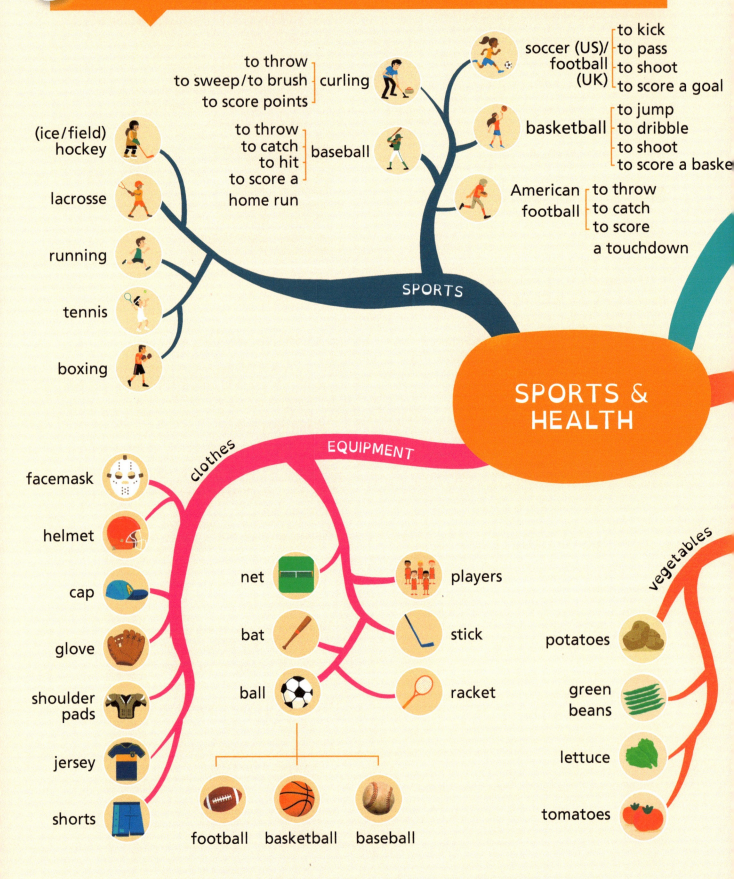

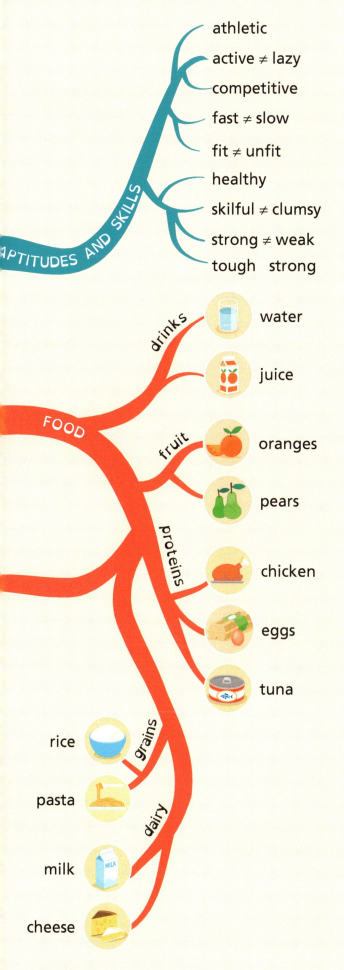

SPORT AND SPORTS EQUIPMENT

1 **Read** the riddles and **identify** the equipment.

a. It is a piece of clothing that covers the top of your body. Your name and number are usually on the back: …

b. You use this piece of wood to hit a baseball: …

c. It protects your head, nose and eyes: …

d. It is a small black disk made of rubber: …

e. You use it to hit the ball, in tennis: …

ABILITIES

2 **Link** each adjective to its opposite.

lazy	clumsy
strong	slow
skilful	active
fast	weak

FOOD

3 **Prepare** a balanced diet for an athlete.

MONDAY	TUESDAY

Create your mind map!
Create your own mind map by choosing the sports, foods and adjective that best correspond to you.

Bloggers 1

eighty-seven 87

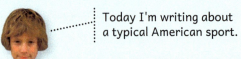

Today I'm writing about a typical American sport.

ARTISTIC AND CULTURAL EDUCATION

 # I ♥ BASEBALL!

I play baseball at school. I love it! Baseball is a national passion in the USA. Baseball is played in other countries too, like Japan and Cuba. My favourite team is the L.A. Dodgers but I also really like the Chicago Cubs.

ERNIE BANKS

Ernie Banks played for the Chicago Cubs from 1953-1971. Some people say he was the best baseball player of all time. This statue is near the entrance of the Cubs stadium. I think it's great!

In the United States, many people like to collect baseball cards with the names and statistics of famous players. Some baseball cards are very rare and they can cost thousands of dollars!

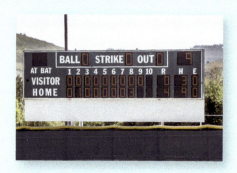

↑ Ernie Banks

Other Posts:
- Multicultural London: India
- Family Paintings
- Two Very Irish Activities
- Tim Burton's Houses
- London Fashion Design
- New York Skyscrapers
- Scottish Legends

Contributors:

 Sheena

 Tom

 Tara

 John

 Kirstine

YOUR TURN!

1 **Read** the text and **find** three countries where people play baseball.

2 What do you collect? Sports cards or something else? **Tell** your partner.

YOU ARE AN ARTIST!
Create your own version of a baseball card: **use** a picture of yourself and **invent** a name, a team, and some statistics (number of games won and lost, number of home runs).

Your challenge

CREATE A POSTER TO PROMOTE YOUR SCHOOL CLUB

Invent a new sport for your American school and look for students to join in.

1. **Write about** your sport: give it a name, explain the rules, the equipment you need.

2. **Invent** a mascot and **choose** your school colours.

3. **Explain** the qualities that your players need to have (tall, fast). **Give** some food recommendations to be a champ.

4. **Include** details about the person to contact, the place where you practise, the days and the time.

5. **Illustrate** your poster. **Make** it attractive, you need to encourage other students to join in!

↓ Digital alternative
You can also create a digital brochure, by using publishing software.

WELCOME TO THE STICKBALL CLUB!

EQUIPMENT
- You need a stick and a ball.

RULES
- There are two teams of eight players each.
- Players must hit the ball into the basket with the stick.

REQUIREMENTS
To play stickball, you need to be fast and strong.

TIPS
To be a stickball champ, you need to eat fruit and vegetables.

CONTACT: Deborah at deb@hotmail.com for more information. We practise on Tuesdays from 5 to 7 pm and the games are on Saturday mornings.

This brand new sport is for you!

To show you have completed this challenge, mark your progress in this unit on the **CHECK YOUR SKILLS** section of your Workbook (p. 97).

Unit 7
New York, New York

What is it that defines New York city?

Tom
Hey Kirstine! Are you ready for the trip? I can't wait for you to come. 8:23

Kirstine
Hi Tom! I'm packing my bag right now. I'm so excited! 8:24

Tom
Me too. I've already prepared an itinerary for you. It includes a visit to the Empire State Building, the Guggenheim Museum, the New York Public Library, Grand Central Station... 8:26

Kirstine
Wow! But hey, I want to relax too! It's my holiday! 8:26

Tom
Ok, don't worry, we can just go to Central Park and sunbathe on the grass with an ice cream. 8:27

Kirstine
Great! 😃 See you soon! 8:27

In this unit, we are going to...
- talk about a trip to Manhattan.
- discover the history of Ellis Island.
- find out more about New York skyscrapers.
- discover the concept of a "melting pot".

Your challenge

Talk about your trip to New York... playing with dice!

Hi, this is **TOM**, from New York City (USA). In this unit you'll learn about the history of NYC.

↑ Central Park in New York City

↑ Tom's vlog

LET'S GO!

1. **Read** Tom and Kirstine's conversation. **Identify** the place names.
2. **Look** at the video still. What do you think it's about?
Imagine a friend is coming to visit you.
Write 4 places you can visit and 4 things you can do.
Compare your list with your partner.

ninety-one **91**

1. Come to NYC!

I can describe my trip to Manhattan.

1 **Watch** Tom's video about Kirstine's trip to New York.
Find the places they mention on the map.
Write 3 places from the video that you want to visit.
Tell your partner and **explain** your choices. WB p. 98

Vocabulary
Vocabulary track: 22

amazing = great = awesome = astonishing
classy
charming
famous = popular
fun
iconic
inspiring
interesting

an avenue = a boulevard
a bridge
a building
a cathedral
a ferry
a harbour
an island
a library
a market
a museum
a park
a restaurant
a skyscraper
a train station

LET'S PLAY...

1. **Listen** to Tom's video and **close** your eyes. **Imagine** a picture that represents the information Tom gives about the 5 places they visit.
2. **Cut** up 5 cards and **write** one place name on the front of each card.
3. **Draw** the picture you imagined on the back of each card.
4. In a group, put all of the cards in a pile. Take it in turns to **take** a card and **show** the group.
5. Each group member **says** the information they think the picture represents.

↑ Mila Studio, **New York Map**

2 **Cover** the postcard Kirstine sent to her family.
In pairs, take it in turns to **read** a paragraph and **imagine** the places.
Cover the postcard again. Take it in turns to **remember** and **say** the places mentioned. WB p. 100

First they went to... Then... Finally...

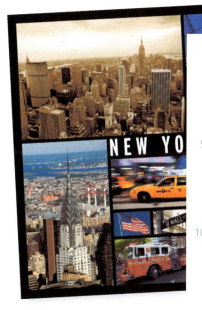

Dear Mum,

This is my first day in New York. It's an amazing city! In New York, there are lots of tall buildings, called skyscrapers. My favourite is the Chrysler Building (you can see it on the postcard). NY has lots of sights like the Statue of Liberty (it was a present from France!).

Tom and I went to Manhattan today. First we visited the American Museum of Natural History (we saw the famous Tyrannosaurus Rex!). It was really awesome. Then we walked around Central Park. There was a zoo in the park! Finally we went to the iconic Fifth Avenue. There were a lot of people, taxis and shops... it was fun! Tomorrow we want to visit Ellis Island.

Miss you, xxx

Kirstine

Did you know?
New York is famous for its cheesecake, bagels, cupcakes, and more... One of my favourite restaurants is Katz's Delicatessen, on the Lower East Side.
It is famous for its pastrami sandwich. The place opened in 1888 and they still use the same recipe!

The past simple

We **went** to Manhattan.
We **visited** the museum.
We **saw** the Tyrannosaurus Rex.
It **was** awesome / fun...

There was a zoo.
There were a lot of people.

MINI CHALLENGE: A TOURIST EXPERIENCE

Friendly Earth is looking for information about different destinations for their world-famous travel guides. WB p. 102

1. **Think about** a tourist experience (it can be real or imaginary).
2. **Take notes** about where you went, what you visited, what it was like.
3. **Record** your presentation and **send** it to Friendly Earth.

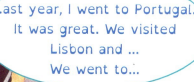

2. The island of hope

I discover the history of Ellis Island.

1 **Read** the texts and **match** them with the sentences.
WB p. 103

a. He arrived in America with no family.
b. She was very sick on the boat.
c. She arrived in America five years after her father.
d. She arrived in Ellis Island in 1910.
e. The journey was awful.

Vocabulary
Vocabulary track: 23

happy ≠ sad
lonely
rough
sick

a beggar
a ship = a boat
tears
a trip = a journey

to arrive in = to get to (→ got)
to be seasick
to come (→ came)
to eat (→ ate)
to feel (→ felt)
to leave (→ left)
to save up money
to say (→ said)
to spend (time) (→ spent)
to take (→ took)
to want

---

1. My father went to America in 1906. Then he saved up money for the tickets to get us over here. He wanted his family. It took five years for him to save up enough money to take us over.
Sonya Kevar, arrived from Russia in 1911, age 13.

2. We spent eleven days on board the ship. The first four days we were deathly sick, seasick, because we were down in the hold. The cheapest possible ticket... I was so sick, and I wanted to die. I was seven years old.
Rota Fichbach, arrived from Germany in 1926, age 7.

3. The trip from Europe was rough. The food was bad. We used to eat like beggars there, we ate sitting on the floor, with our plates next to us. White tin plates.
Tessie Croce, arrived from Italy in 1912, age 15.

4. Do you know how I felt when I left my home, my father and my mother? Terrible, terrible. That's how I felt. I was the first in my family to come.
Theodore Spake, arrived from Greece in 1911, age 16.

5. When we got to America, we saw the Statue of Liberty, and Mother said to me, "That means we are free." I remember her saying that. And to this day I think I'm a better American than a lot of them born here, because when I sing 'God Bless America' I'm in tears.
Margaret Wertle, arrived from Hungary in 1910, age 7.

↑ Louise Peacock, **At Ellis Island: A History in Many Voices**

↑ Statue of Liberty, New York City

2 **Watch** part 2 of Tom's video about their visit to the old immigration station.
Identify the different parts of the journey. WB p. 104

CITIZENSHIP

Melting pot

Look at the picture.
Can you explain it?

3 **Listen to** the Ellis Island audio guide.
Track: 11
Find the names of rooms 1, 2, 3, 4
Take notes about each step of the visit.
WB p. 105

Vocabulary
Vocabulary track: 24

dangerous
difficult
poor ≠ rich

a bag ≈ baggage
belongings = personal objects
an immigrant
a prison
to be free
to be married
to become (→ became)
to have money
to interview
to return

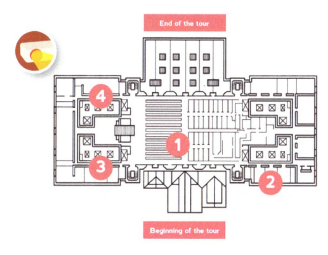

Time markers
In 1906… / **From** 1880 **to** 1930…
100 years **ago**…
In the past…
In those days…

MINI CHALLENGE: AN IMMIGRANT'S STORY

Write about an immigrant's story. WB p. 107

1 **Read** the information about an immigrant's voyage to Ellis Island.

2 **Imagine** her name, her country of origin, the people she travelled with, her feelings.

3 **Write** a text about her experience in the first person (I…). You can **add** information.

- leave her village (March 1900)
- board the boat (April 1900)
- cross the ocean (2 weeks)
- see the Statue of Liberty (26th June morning)
- arrive in Ellis Island (26th June afternoon)

I left Italy
five months ago…

Bloggers 1

My grammar ⇢ Exercises p. 120

I understand and I practise.

1. THE PAST TENSE OF TO BE

Use the past simple tense to talk about the past.

- To be is the only verb that has two forms in the past tense (singular and plural).

POSITIVE FORM		
I / He / She	was	very poor at the time.
You / We / They	were	very poor at the time.

- Use it with there to talk about something in the past tense.
  there was / were indicates that something existed in the past.

  There was a zoo.
  There were a lot of people.

2. FORMING THE PAST SIMPLE TENSE
WB p. 100

In English, regular verbs are different from irregular verbs.

- To make the past tense with a regular verb, add -ed to the verb root.
  visit → visited

- For verbs that end in -e: add -d to the verb root.
  arrive → arrived

- For verbs that end in a consonant + -y:
  y is replaced by i.
  cry → cried

- For verbs that end in a vocal and a consonant, repeat the final consonant.
  stop → stopped

Pronunciation ⇢ WB p. 110
The pronunciation of "-ed "

Irregular verbs that need to be learnt by heart.

become → became
come → came
do → did
eat → ate
feel → felt
get → got
go → went

have → had
leave → left
make → made
say → said
see → saw
spend → spent
take → took

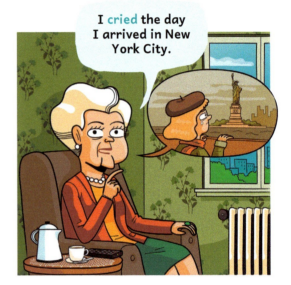

1 Write these verbs in the past simple tense.
a. like → liked
b. carry
c. play
d. wait
e. dance
f. cross
g. board
h. believe
i. marry
j. look

2 Complete the sentences below by writing the verbs in the past simple tense.
a. My uncle .... (visit) us last weekend.
b. Yesterday I .... (listen) to Italian music.
c. We .... (study) hard for the history exam.
d. I .... (wait) for the school bus for 20 minutes.
e. Yesterday night, somebody .... (knock) at the door.
f. The bus .... (be) full so we .... (walk) to the museum.
g. Her father .... (be) sick when they .... (arrive) in Ellis Island.

3. TIME MARKERS FOR THE PAST TENSE WB p. 106

Time markers are words (or phrases) that specify when an action takes place. Here are some time markers for the past tense:

`(day/week/month/year) + ago`

I went to New York two years ago.

`yesterday`

Yesterday I visited the MoMa, the Museum of Modern Art.

`last + noun (week/night/month/year)`

Last year I went to New York.

`in + date/period of time`

In 1910, a lot of people arrived in New York.

In those days / In the past, New York was a rough city.

`from... (date/period of time) to... (date/period of time)`

From 1880 to 1930, 12 million immigrants arrived in the USA.

`first / then / finally`

First, we visited the American Museum of Natural History.
Then, we walked around Central Park.
Finally, we went to the Fifth Avenue.

> Think about the word **ago**. Is there an equivalent time marker in your language? Where is it placed in the sentence?

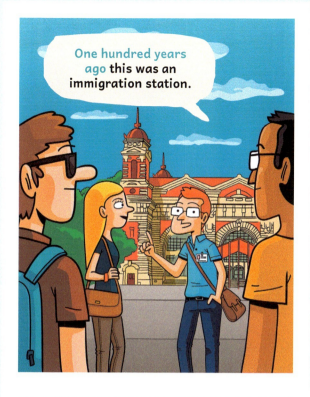

One hundred years ago this was an immigration station.

3 Complete these sentences with the appropriate time markers.

a. He lived in Washington .... 1998 .... 2016.
b. .... 1980 there were fewer people in NYC.
c. .... week I went to the American Museum of Natural History.
d. I was in Brooklyn two years .... .
e. My grand-parents lived in the United States .... 1973 .... 1984.
f. .... 1984, they left the United States and settled in Europe.

4 Put these events in the right order.

a. We went to our hotel in Manhattan. ....
b. We left home. ....
c. We arrived in New York. ....
d. We visited Grand Central Station. ....
e. We went to the airport. ....
f. It was great! ....

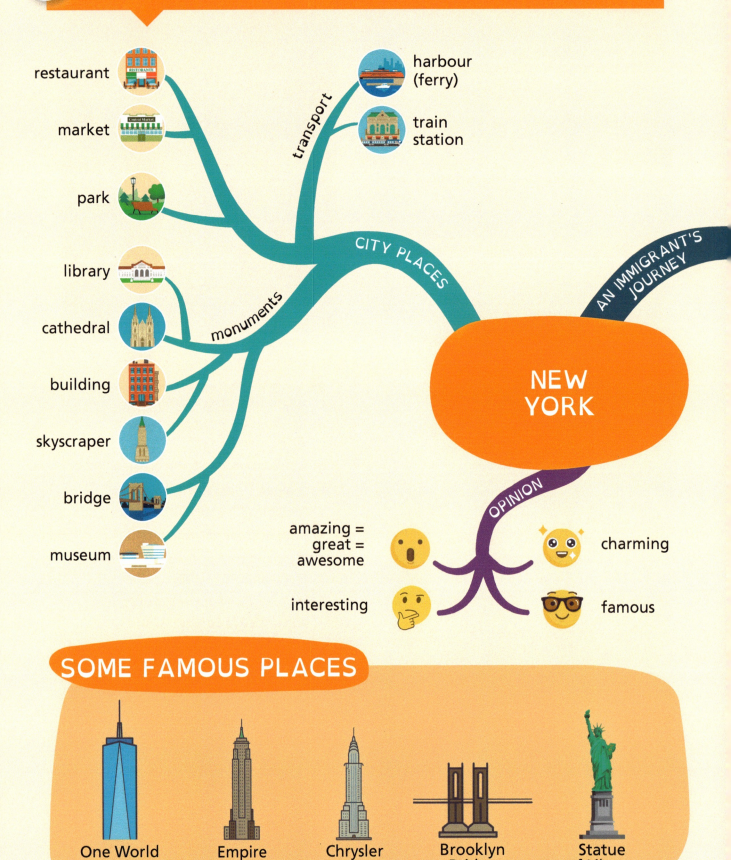

PLACES IN A CITY

1 **Match** each action with the corresponding place.

take a train	museum
walk around	train station
take a boat	hospital
cross a river	bridge
see a doctor	harbour
learn about history	park

TRAVELLING AND FEELINGS

2 **Complete** each sentence with an adjective. There are many possible answers.

a. I really liked the trip to NYC; it was ….!
b. I was …. to leave the country after such good holidays.
c. I was alone at home, I felt …. before coming to this big city full of people everywhere.
d. I was really …. to come and meet you for the first time, you're so nice.
e. It was quite …. at the beginning to find my way in this country.

3 **Find** the odd one out. **Justify** your choice.

a. poverty   freedom   oppression   war

b. library   cathedral   museum   park

c. interesting   charming   rough   awesome

Create your mind map!
Create a mind map for the different places in your town/village and explain what you think about the place.

Bloggers 1

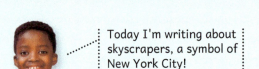

Today I'm writing about skyscrapers, a symbol of New York City!

ARTISTIC AND CULTURAL EDUCATION

NEW YORK SKYSCRAPERS

People worked in very dangerous situations to build skyscrapers!

Other Posts:
- Multicultural London
- Family Paintings
- Two Very Irish Activities
- Tim Burton's Houses
- London Fashion Design
- I Love Baseball
- Scottish Legends

Contributors:

 Sheena

 Tom

 Tara

 John

 Kirstine

I love the skyscrapers in New York! They are tall buildings (more than 50m high) with multiple floors, at least 40 to 50 floors! Can you imagine? A lot of people work in there. Some especially tall skyscrapers (300 metres high) are called 'supertall'.

The most famous skyscrapers in the United States are on the island of Manhattan: the Empire State Building, the Chrysler Building and the One World Trade Center (or 1WTC). They are very popular destinations. The 1WTC was finished in 2013, and it is the tallest building in North America.

YOUR TURN!

1 **List** the different New York City skyscrapers in the text. Do you know any other skyscrapers that are in another city?

2 The 1WTC replaced another famous building that disappeared in 2001. Do you know its name? What happened in 2001?

YOU ARE AN ARTIST!
Create a poster to compare the sizes of famous buildings.
Look for information on the Internet: how tall are the skyscrapers in Tom's text? And how tall is the Eiffel Tower?
Now you can **present** your information in a visual form.

Your challenge

TELL YOUR STORY ABOUT NEW YORK

Imagine that you went to New York...
Roll the dice and tell your story!

1. **Divide** the class into three groups.
2. Each group **cuts out** four dice shapes and **writes**:
   a. places you visited in New York.
   b. when you went.
   c. who you went with.
   d. your opinion about the trip.
3. **Glue** the four dice into cubes.
4. Each group **picks** two students to be judges.
5. Each student **rolls** the full set of dice and **tells** their story.
6. The judges **give** points (1 to 5) to each student.
7. The first team to **reach** 25 points is the winner!

↓ **Digital alternative**
Record your story about New York with audio editing software.

On Monday I visited the Empire State Building. I remember the views from the top were awesome. It was great!

To show you have completed this challenge, mark your progress in this unit on the **CHECK YOUR SKILLS** section of your Workbook (p. 111).

Unit 8
A trip to Scotland

What are the main attractions in Scotland?

Tom
Hi Kirstine! What's the weather like today in Glasgow? It's sunny here in New York. 12:52

Kirstine
Not bad. At least it isn't raining. And summer is coming soon. By the way, where are you going for your summer holidays? 12:53

Tom
I'll probably go to Florida with my parents. What about you? 12:54

Kirstine
Maybe we'll go to the Highlands. That's in the north of Scotland, not very far from Glasgow. 12:54

Tom
What will you do in the Highlands? 12:55

Kirstine
I suppose we'll visit some castles, see some lochs... I'm excited! 12:55

Tom
Have a great time!   12:56

→ In this unit, we are going to...
- talk about tours and the weather in Scotland.
- organise holiday activities in Glasgow.
- discover two Scottish legends.
- talk about environmentally friendly means of transport.

Your challenge
To organise a four-day tour around Scotland.

Hi, I'm **KIRSTINE**, from Glasgow (Scotland). In this unit you'll learn about my country.

↑ Castle in ruins on the shore of Loch Ness

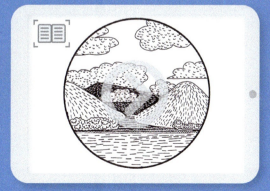

↑ Kristine's vlog

LET'S GO!

1. **Read** Kirstine's conversation.
   Correct these sentences with a partner.
   a. It's raining in Glasgow.
   b. Tom will go to California in the summer.
   c. The Highlands are in the south of Scotland.

2. **Look** at the picture from Kirstine's video.
   Choose words to describe Scotland.

one hundred and three **103**

1. We'll visit Loch Ness!

I can talk about tourist routes and the weather in Scotland.

1 **Watch** part 1 of Kirstine's video. **Complete** the names of the tours. **Match** the texts to the correct photo. WB p. 112

MAGIC a) ... TOUR

This five-day Scotland tour through the **Highlands** will take you to spectacular scenery where you'll have some unforgettable experiences.
5 You'll go monster hunting in **Loch Ness**, ride the Jacobite train to the capital, **Inverness**, and explore the impressive mountains around **Glencoe**. Get ready to connect with
10 nature!

PEACE & b) ... TOUR

Take this three-day tour to explore the romantic **Isle of Skye**. You'll hike a 50-mile-long path among spectacular moors, mountains, lochs,
5 waterfalls and sea cliffs. You'll also find many castles, museums, and art galleries. But mostly, you'll enjoy the peace and quiet of this island of colourful houses.

CULTURE & c) ... TOUR

This tour will start in the wonderful city of **Edinburgh**, a wonderful city. We'll spend three days visiting the castle, the Scottish National Gallery, and the
5 Princess Street Gardens. Then we'll continue up to **Stirling Castle**. On day five, we'll get to **Loch Lomond** to enjoy some water activities such as swimming and kayaking. We'll
10 travel back south to finish our tour in **Glasgow**, the city of culture and architecture.

2 **Watch** part 1 of Kirstine's video again. **Say** which tour you think Jim and Lisa will choose and why. WB p. 113

> I think that they will take the... tour because...

3 **Imagine** you have decided to visit Scotland. **Choose** one tour and **justify**.

> Personally, I would love to take...

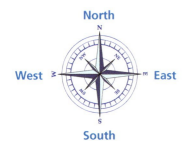

Vocabulary
Vocabulary track: 25

impressive
romantic
spectacular
unforgettable
wonderful

a castle
a cliff
an island
a loch (lake)
a moor

a mountain
a river
a waterfall

to enjoy
to explore
to go kayaking
to go sightseeing
to hike
to ride a train

Future: *will*

We **will** (**we'll**) visit a castle.
You **will not** (**won't**) miss the famous castle.

4 **Listen to** a weather forecast. **Place** the symbols and the temperatures on the map. WB p. 116

Track: 13

↑ Mila Studio, **Map of Scotland**

Vocabulary
Vocabulary track: 26

 cloudy
 rainy ≠ dry
 snowy
 sunny
 windy
 a shower
 a thunderstorm
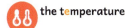 the temperature

LET'S PLAY...

The secret word game
1. Two contestants **stand** in front of the board.
2. Another student **writes** a word from this unit on the board so the contestants can't see.
3. Contestants **take turns** to ask classmates for clues to the secret word.
4. The contestant who **guesses** the secret word **stays** in front of the board.
5. The student who **gives** the last clue **replaces** the other contestant.

MINI CHALLENGE: A LEAFLET ABOUT YOUR COUNTRY (group work)

WORLDTOURS4U IS LAUNCHING TWO-DAY TOURS IN YOUR COUNTRY.
DESIGN THE LEAFLET FOR A TOUR. WB p. 117

1 **Choose** a type of tour (nature, adventure, history).
2 **Look for** four places to visit / things to do. **Look** this lesson and on the Internet.
3 **Organise** the activities across two days.
4 **Find** some great pictures.
5 Each student in the group **writes** a text for each place to explain what visitors will do and see on one day. **Include** information about the weather.
6 **Design** your leaflet and include the pictures and the texts.

2. Let's go to Glasgow!

I can organise holiday activities in Glasgow.

1 **Watch** part 2 of Kirstine's video.
Find the places they visit on the map.
Write the missing information. WB p. 118
Answer the questions.

a. Where will you go if you want to see great paintings?
b. Where can you go on a Saturday at 9:30 am?
c. What can you visit every day from 9.45 am to 5.15 pm?
d. Where will you go if you like vehicles?
e. What will you see if you visit the Lighthouse?
f. Where will you go if you want to go shopping?

Vocabulary
Vocabulary track: 27

an art gallery
a cathedral /
the city centre
an entrance fee
an exhibition

a lighthouse /
a museum /
opening hours /
a shopping area /

If... will

If you go to Kelvingrove, you will see great art.

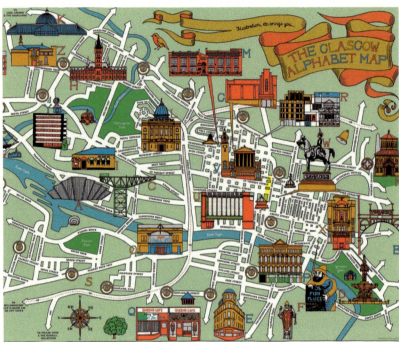

Rosemary Cunningham, The Glasgow Alphabet Map

School of Art

Glasgow cathedral   Buchanan Street

Kelvingrove Museum

Riverside Museum   Lighthouse

Botanic Gardens

1 The **Lighthouse** is a centre for design and architecture. It contains original objects, interactive touch screens and architectural models.
Opening hours: Monday-Saturday 10.30am-5pm/ Sunday 12pm-5pm
Entrance fee: a) ...

2 **Kelvingrove Art Gallery and Museum** is one of Scotland's most popular free attractions. It houses one of Europe's best art collections (Dalí, Rembrandt, Van Gogh, Gauguin and more).
Opening hours: Monday-Thursday & Saturday 10am-5pm/ Friday & Sunday b) ...
Entrance fee: free entry

3 At the **Glasgow School of Art**, one of the masterpieces of Charles Rennie Mackintosh, Scotland's most famous architect, you will discover Glasgow's creative past and present through design.
Opening hours: 7 days 9.45am-5.15pm
Entrance fee: c) ...

4 The d) ... houses some of the world's finest vehicles, including boats, cars, skateboards and bikes.
Opening hours: Monday-Thursday & Saturday 10am-5pm/ Friday & Sunday 11am-5pm
Entrance fee: free entry

5 The **Glasgow cathedral** is one of Scotland's most magnificent medieval buildings and a fantastic way to travel back in time.
Opening hours: Monday-Saturday 9.30am e) .../Sunday 1pm-5pm
Entrance fee: free entry

6 The **Botanic Gardens** is located in the West End of Glasgow. It's the best garden in the city, and it houses the national collection of tree ferns.
Opening hours: 7 days 7am-6pm
Entrance fee: free entry

7 **Buchanan Street** is a pedestrian boulevard lined with beautiful buildings and some of the city's finest shops.

2 Listen to Naomi, an American tourist, calling the Tourist Information Office in Glasgow. **Write** her itinerary and the transport she will take.
Track: 14
WB p. 119

Naomi will visit...

 School of Art ☐
 Glasgow cathedral ☐
 Lighthouse ☐
 Botanic Gardens ☐

 Buchanan Street ☐
 Riverside Museum ☐
 Kelvingrove Museum ☐

 Did you know?
The name 'Glasgow' comes from a Gaelic phrase meaning 'green valley' or 'dear green place'. Scottish Gaelic is an old Celtic language, very different from English.

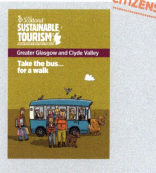

CITIZENSHIP

Eco-friendly transport

1. Look at the picture. What can you see?

2. Which means of transport are more eco-friendly?

 Visit Scotland, **Sustainable Tourism**

Vocabulary — Vocabulary track: 28

What are the **o**pening hours?
How much does it cost?
How can I get there?
Is it worth g**o**ing?
Is it worth v**i**siting?

Time expressions

She will visit the Cathedral **before** she goes to the Riverside Museum.

Making suggestions

Why don't we...?
What about...?
How about...?
Let's...!

LET'S PLAY...

The future tense chain game (group work)
1. A student **invents** a sentence about the future.
2. The next student **says** a new sentence that includes the last part of the previous one, and so on.

If I go on holiday, I will go to Scotland.

If I go to Scotland, I will...

 MINI CHALLENGE: 24 HOURS IN GLASGOW (pair work)

STUDENT A: You are a tourist in Glasgow. WB p. 123

1 **Choose** two places from the list of places in Glasgow.
2 **Tell** student B your choices.
3 **Prepare** questions to ask about: the price, the opening hours, the means of transport, what you will be able to do or see there.

STUDENT B: You work at Glasgow's Tourist Information Office.

1 **Read** the leaflet about Glasgow.
2 **Write down** information for each place: the price, the opening hours, the exact location, what you can do or see there.
3 **Prepare** your answers to student A.
4 **Role play!**

Hello! Can I help you?

Yes, please! I want to go to...

My grammar ⇢ Exercises p. 121

I understand and I practise.

1. WILL + INFINITIVE WB p. 115

Use *will* for these situations:
- Decision in the moment: *I'm hungry. I think I will buy a sandwich.*
- Offer: *That looks heavy. I will help you carry it.*
- Promise: *You will love the castle.*
- Prediction: *There are a lot of clouds. It will rain soon.*
- Refusal: *He won't listen to anything you say.*

Note! You can use contractions:

I will = I'll   It will = it'll
You will = you'll   We will = we'll
She will = she'll   They will = they'll
He will = he'll

1 Answer the questions below.
a. Will it rain tomorrow? ...
b. Do you think you will have pizza for dinner? ...
c. What **won't** you do when you're tired? ...

2 Say what the weather will be like in Britain tomorrow.

Pronunciation ⇢ WB p. 126
The pronunciation of **will**
Intonation at the phrase level

2. THE FIRST CONDITIONAL (IF... WILL) WB p. 121

Structure:
if + present simple + will / won't + infinitive verb

Situation: To talk about possibility **now** or in the **future**.

Example: *If I visit Scotland, I will go to Glasgow.*
If we go to the loch, we won't have time to see the lighthouse.

Notice! You can invert first conditional sentences, just remove the comma!

Example: *If I visit Scotland, I will go to Glasgow.*

→ *I will go to Glasgow if I visit Scotland.*

3 Complete the sentences below with the correct form of the verb shown in brackets.
a. If I ... (go) to Scotland, I ... (visit) Loch Ness.
b. I ... (not be) happy if I ... (not see) Edinburgh Castle.
c. If he ... (come) to Glasgow, I ... (take) him to Loch Lomond.
d. If it ... (rain), they ... (not go) to the Isle of Skye.
e. If I ... (visit) Scotland this summer, I ... (have) two weeks to see the country.
f. She ... (take) a taxi if she ... (be) tired after the visit.

4 If you have £500, what will you do? **Look** at the drawings and **write** a sentence for each one.

3. TIME EXPRESSIONS WB p. 122

Use time expressions to talk about **when** actions happen.

Structure: will + infinitive verb + time expression + present simple

Example: *I'll go* to Glasgow *before* she goes to Edinburgh.

1 Glasgow roadsign   2 Edinburgh roadsign

Example: *We'll visit* the loch *after* they see the castle.

1 castle   2 a lake

5 Choose the correct form of the verb.
a. I'll prepare the picnic before you **come/'ll come**.
b. When you get up, we **go/'ll go** kayaking.
c. After we visit the Botanic Gardens, Kirstine's dad **drives/will drive** us to the lake.
d. Don't worry! I'll watch you carefully when you **go/will go** for a swim in the lake.

4. SUGGESTIONS WB p. 122

To suggest an activity… you can use these options:

- Let's…

  Let's + infinitive verb

  Let's go to the mall today.

- Using a question:

  How about + verb-ing?
  What about + verb-ing?

  How about watching a movie this weekend?

  Why don't we + infinitive verb

Why don't we go to the park this afternoon?

6 Write the suggestions below with phrases from the *Suggestions* box.
a. We can relax in Victoria park.
b. We can taste some traditional Scottish food.
c. We can discover wonderful landscapes in the Highlands.
d. We can write a travel blog to share our experiences.
e. We can take a picture in front of the castle.

7 You go on a trip to Scotland with some friends. Suggest the four activities below.

1

2

3

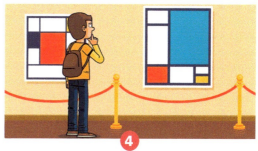

4

My vocabulary

→ Exercises, p. 121
→ WB p. 124

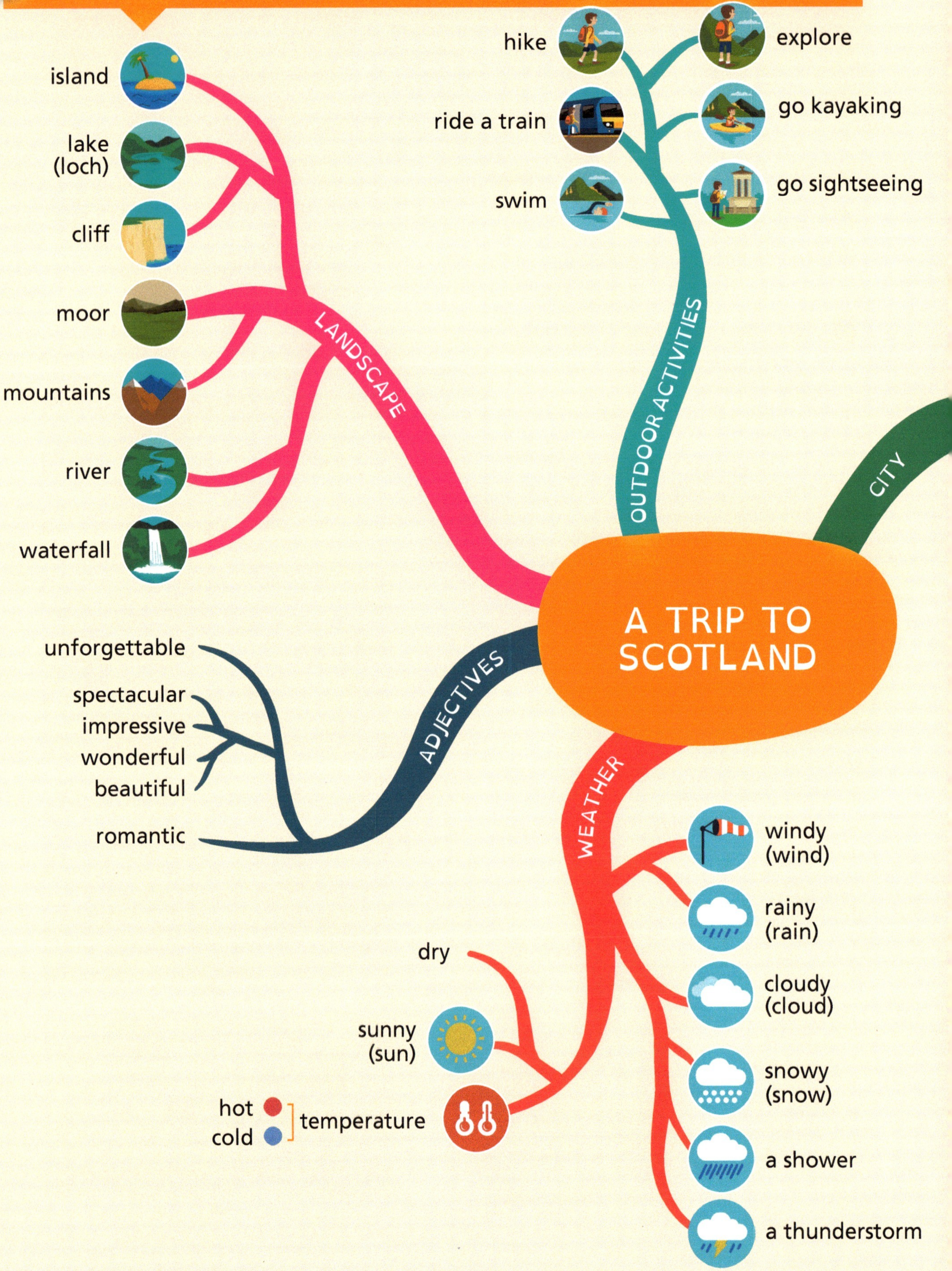

I see and I memorise.

A TRIP TO SCOTLAND

LANDSCAPE
- island
- lake (loch)
- cliff
- moor
- mountains
- river
- waterfall

OUTDOOR ACTIVITIES
- hike
- explore
- ride a train
- go kayaking
- swim
- go sightseeing

CITY

ADJECTIVES
- unforgettable
- spectacular
- impressive
- wonderful
- beautiful
- romantic

WEATHER
- windy (wind)
- rainy (rain)
- cloudy (cloud)
- snowy (snow)
- a shower
- a thunderstorm
- dry
- sunny (sun)
- temperature: hot, cold

110 one hundred and ten

Bloggers 1

OUTDOOR ACTIVITIES AND THE LANDSCAPE

1 Find the odd one out in each list.
a. lake — moor — waterfall — river
b. go kayaking — swim — hike

ADJECTIVES

2 Which adjectives would you use to describe these places?
a. a place you will always remember: ....
b. a place you choose to tell someone you love him/her: ....

THE WEATHER

3 Complete the sentences below.
a. Kirstine is wearing sunglasses because it is ....
b. Tomorrow, it will be very ...., the temperature will be around -5°C.
c. It is very .... today, I hope it doesn't rain.
d. Don't forget your umbrella, it will be .... all day.
e. There are high temperatures, the weather will be .... .

THE CITY

4 Complete the sentences below.
a. If you visit the ...., you will see beautiful paintings.
b. Kings and queens lived in this .... before.
c. I have to buy a ...., I am completely lost.
d. You can have a picnic in the .... .
e. Very often, the tourist information office is in the .... .
f. You don't have to pay an .... to visit the cathedral.

MEANS OF TRANSPORT

5 Find 4 means of transport and 3 landmarks.

BAYWUS — DREHACLAT — RODUEDRGUNN — RALYGLE — RTIAN — CLESAT — ARC

Create your mind map!
Create a mind map for your perfect holiday: choose the words that correspond to your favourite activities, your perfect weather, your favourite places, etc.

Today I'm writing about two Scottish legends.

SCOTTISH LEGENDS

Scotland is a land of myths and legends. Here are two examples I like!

THE SALMON AND THE RING

The city of Glasgow is represented by a coat of arms. There is a salmon with a ring in its mouth. Can you guess why?

A long time ago, a Scottish queen gave a ring to a soldier. The king discovered this and he was furious! He met the soldier by a river, took the ring and threw it in the water. The legend says that St Mungo caught a salmon and miracuously found the ring in its stomach. Today, St Mungo is the patron saint of Glasgow. Some people think that he protects the city!

↑ Glasgow's Coat of Arms, as featured on the Kelvin Bridge

THE LOCH NESS MONSTER

Loch Ness is a huge, beautiful lake, but the reason so many people come to visit the place is... the Loch Ness monster!

The legend of a monster that looks like a dinosaur the lake is very well-known. Many explorers and scientists have tried to find scientific evidence of the monster. Some people say that they have photographs of it! In reality, it is only a legend, but in Scotland we like our "monster"... It even has a nickname: Nessie.

Other Posts:
- Multicultural London: India
- Family Paintings
- Two Very Irish Activities
- Tim Burton's Houses
- London Fashion Design
- I Love Baseball
- New York Skyscrapers

Contributors:

 Sheena

 Tom

 Tara

 John

 Kirstine

YOUR TURN!

1 **Look** at the pictures, **read** the texts and **answer** the questions.
   a. What part of each legend shows that nature is very important in Scotland?
   b. Does the Loch Ness monster really exist?
   c. Who was St Mungo?

YOU ARE AN ARTIST!
Create your own Nessie: **draw** it, **paint** it or **make** it with parts of a magazine.

Your challenge

PLAN A TRIP TO SCOTLAND

Student A: You decide to go to Scotland this summer for four days.

1. **Take notes** about the activities you would like to do (culture, adventure) and the places you'd like to see (cities, lakes, castles).
2. **Give** your notes to student B.
3. **Call** your penfriend on Skype and **agree** on an itinerary.
4. Don't forget to **make** your own **suggestions** and to **ask questions** about the places.

Student B: You are Scottish. Help your penfriend organise their four-day trip to Scotland.

1. **Read** your penfriend's notes.
2. **Prepare** a tour for them based on their preferences.
3. **Call** your penfriend on Skype and **suggest** the itinerary.
4. Be ready to **give information** about the weather, the means of transport, etc.

> I'll meet you at the airport and then we'll go to the city centre by train. There, we'll...

> If the weather is good, we will...

> That's fine but do you think we'll go to see "Nessie"?

↓Digital alternative

Use your mobile phones, or talk on Skype or a similar app for long distance communications. It will make your conversation more realistic.

To show you have completed this challenge, mark your progress in this unit on the **CHECK YOUR SKILLS** section of your Workbook (p. 127).

Exercises

Unit 1 New school, new life

SUBJECT PRONOUNS

1 Complete the phrase with the correct subject pronoun.

a. • Where are ..... from? o ..... am from Belgium.

b. Hi, ... are Samuel and David.

c. • Kate and Brian, are ..... 12? o Yes, ... are.

QUESTION WORDS (1)

2 Write the questions for each answer

a. .....? I speak French of course but I also speak English.

b. .....? I live in Spain.

c. .....? I'm 11 years old.

d. .....? My birthday is on 10th July.

3 An English-speaking student arrives in your class. **Write** questions to ask her.

a. You want to know her name.

b. You think she is twelve years old but you are not sure.

c. You think she is British.

d. You want to know where she is from exactly.

THE PRESENT SIMPLE TENSE OF THE VERB TO BE (1)

4 Complete the sentences below with the full form of the verb to be, or the affirmative or negative form.

a. We ..... from the USA. ✗

b. You ..... Australian. ✓

c. I ..... 13 years old. ✗

d. We ..... Todd and Simon. ✓

e. You ..... a headteacher. ✗

f. I ..... bilingual. ✓

EXPRESSING LIKES AND DISLIKES

5 Write down two activities that you:
- **love** doing
- **like** doing
- **don't** like doing
- **hate** doing

ARTICLES: A / AN, THE AND THE ZERO ARTICLE

6 Complete the sentences below with a / an, the or Ø.

Welcome to my school! This is (1) ..... playground. (2) ..... computer room is next to (3) ..... hall. (4) ..... cafeteria is between (5) ..... lab and (6) ..... theatre. There is also (7) ..... art room and (8) ..... big library. It's fantastic. I love to read (9) ..... books.

POSSESSIVE ADJECTIVES

7 Complete the sentences below with a subject pronoun (I, you…) or a possessive adjective (my, your…). **Check** if the word that follows is a verb or a noun.

Hello! (1) ..... 'm Sara and this is (2) ..... friend Amanda. (3) ..... are both eleven. (4) ..... are British. (5) ..... love to play sports in (6) ..... school club. Tell us about yourself. What's (7) ..... name? How old are (8) .....? What sports do (9) ..... like?

COUNTRIES, NATIONALITIES AND LANGUAGES

8 Complete the sentences below with the correct country, nationality or language.

a. I am from ..... . I am British. I speak ..... .

b. We are from France. We are ..... .

c. They are from China. They are ..... .

d. I am from ..... . I am Algerian.

e. We are from Germany. We are ..... .

f. You are from ..... . You are American. You speak ..... .

Unit 2 American family

THE VERB HAVE GOT

1 **Choose** between **have** and **has**.

a. We have / has got two cars: a Ford and an Audi.
b. Sometimes our teachers haven't / hasn't got a lot of patience with us!
c. Have / Has you got a mobile phone?
d. My sister have / has got a strange boyfriend; I don't like him.
e. We have / has got a long holiday in summer.
f. I haven't / hasn't got a TV in my bedroom.
g. My best friend have / has got an exam tomorrow.
h. Have / Has he got a girlfriend?

THE PRESENT SIMPLE TENSE OF THE VERB TO BE (2)

2 **Complete** the sentences about Ding.

he's | are | they (x 2) | his (x 2) | is | he

This (1) ..... Ding. (2) ..... 12 years old. And this is (3) ..... father. (4) ..... are from China but now (5) ..... live in England. (6) ..... bilingual, he speaks Chinese and English. He and (7) ..... father love football. Their favourite team is Manchester United. They (8) ..... big fans of Barcelona too.

ADJECTIVE POSITION

3 **Rewrite** the sentences below. Put the adjective in brackets in the correct place.

a. Her / voice / is / . (beautiful)
b. We / live / in / a / house / . (new)
c. Our / dog / is / so / ! (intelligent)
d. My / mother / has / got / eyes / . (brown)
e. We / have / got / two / cats / . (black)
f. He / has / got / hair / . (long)

THE FAMILY

4 **Find** the odd one out in each group. **Explain** your choice.

a.
- sister
- brother
- wife
- aunt

b.
- uncle
- daughter
- grandfather
- nephew

c.
- half-sister
- cousin
- stepmother
- half-brother

d.
- father
- sister
- brother
- cousin

DESCRIBING PHYSICAL CHARACTERISTICS

5 **Complete** the descriptions by using the adjectives below.

blonde | blue | hair | long
pretty | soft | eyes | thin

Margaret, the eldest of the four, is sixteen, and very (1) ..... . She has got big (2) ..... , brown (3) ..... , a sweet mouth, and white hands.

Fifteen-year-old Jo is very tall and (4) ..... . She has got beautiful (5) ..... brown hair. And she has got big hands and feet.

Elizabeth, or Beth, as everyone calls her, is thirteen. She has got bright eyes, (6) ..... hair, a shy manner and a timid voice.

Amy, though the youngest, is a most important person, in her own opinion at least. She has got (7) ..... eyes, and (8) ..... hair.

Exercises

Unit 3 My week

THE PRESENT SIMPLE TENSE

1 Complete the text with the following words.

In the morning I **(1)** ..... at 7 o'clock. I **(2)** ..... my face and **(3)** ..... my teeth. Then, I **(4)** ..... breakfast. I usually **(5)** ..... milk or fruit juice, but I never **(6)** ..... tea. After breakfast I **(7)** ..... my schoolbag and say 'Have a good day' to my parents. I **(8)** ..... home at 8 o'clock.

2 Rewrite the sentences in exercise 1 with **she** as the subject. Remember to change the form of the possessive adjectives.

3 Match the words in each column to ask questions. Then, answer them.

a. Do you sometimes cook…
b. Does your mother play…
c. Do your parents drink…
d. Do you…

1. have a mobile phone?
2. tea for breakfast?
3. dinner at home?
4. video games in the evening?

TIME EXPRESSIONS

4 Choose the correct preposition for each example.

Sean always goes to his judo club **(1)** in/on/at Wednesday. The club opens **(2)** in/on/at the afternoon and the lesson starts **(3)** in/on/at two o'clock. **(4)** In/On/At Sunday, Sean has competitions. He has to get up **(5)** in/on/at seven thirty because the competitions are always **(6)** in/on/at the morning. Poor Sean! No lie-in **(7)** in/on/at Sunday.

ADVERBS OF FREQUENCY

5 Rewrite the sentences below by putting the frequency adverb in brackets in the correct place.

a. We go to Corsica for our holidays but not this year. (**usually**)
b. When there's a birthday in my family we have lunch together. (**sometimes**)
c. My mother helps me with my homework. (**never**) I do it alone. (**always**)
d. My parents get up at 6.30 am – even at the weekend! (**always**)

QUESTION WORDS (2)

6 Complete these questions with the correct question word.

a. • ..... does the first lesson begin? ○ At 8 o'clock.
b. • ..... does he usually have for lunch? ○ Rice and fish.
c. • ..... do you have the longest holidays? ○ In summer.
d. • ..... do you go to school? ○ By bus.
e. • ..... wants to sing this song? ○ Tamara.

SCHOOL SUBJECTS

7 Put the letters in the correct order to find 6 school subjects.

8 Complete the sentences below with a school subject.

a. In ..... class, I learn to play the flute.
b. In ..... class, I work with numbers.
c. In ..... class, we learn to draw and paint.
d. We study plants, animals and life in ..... class.
e. We learn about the past in ..... class.
f. Our ..... teacher helps us learn this language.

Unit 4 Home, sweet home

THERE IS / THERE ARE

1 Complete the sentences below.

a. There ..... two kitchens in our new house.
b. There ..... a sofa in my bedroom.
c. There ..... two dogs in the garden.
d. There ..... five chairs in the dining room.
e. There ..... a big garage too!

THE POSSESSIVE FORM

2 Underline the possessive 's.

Hello, I'm Marie. I live in Los Angeles. I live with my parents and my sister, Alice. We have a dog. In fact, it's Alice's dog, but I take care of him too.
His name is Bin.
Bin's a very cute dog.
He's always sleeping or playing with us.
I like Alice's dog a lot.

THE NEGATIVE FORM OF THE VERB HAVE GOT

3 Write these sentences in the negative form.

a. I have got a big bedroom.
b. They have got three bathrooms in their house.
c. We have got a computer in our bedroom.
d. She has got a new friend.

HOW MANY?

4 Ask questions for these answers.

a. I have three bedrooms in my house.
b. They have two bedrooms in their house.
c. She has two best friends.
d. We have two little brothers.

OBJECT PRONOUNS

5 Complete the sentences below with an object pronoun.

a. I like swimming with my friends.
   I like swimming with ..... .
b. They always play football with my father.
   They always play football with ..... .
c. I like going to school with my mother.
   I like going to school with ..... .

OBLIGATION AND PROHIBITION

6 Place these phrases in the correct table column.

take out the trash | clean my room | play in the kitchen

watch TV all day | do the washing up | clean the table

AT HOME I MUST...	AT HOME I MUSTN'T...

ROOMS IN A HOUSE

7 Complete the sentences below with the correct location.

bathroom | kitchen | garden | living room

a. Tom plays football in the ..... .
b. Dad cooks in the ..... .
c. Donna watches TV in the ..... .
d. My parents have a ..... inside their bedroom.

PREPOSITIONS OF PLACE

8 Complete the sentences below with the correct preposition.

a. The ball is ..... the table.
b. The ball is ..... the table.
c. The ball is ..... the table.
d. The ball is ..... the tables.
e. The ball is ..... the table.

Exercises

Unit 5 Looking good!

EXPRESSING PERMISSION WITH CAN / CAN'T

1 **Write** sentences to say if you can/can't wear these items of clothing to school.

a. b. c.

d. e. f.

THE PRESENT CONTINUOUS

2 **Complete** the sentences below with the present simple or present continuous form of the word in brackets.

a. We can't go to the park today because it ..... (**rain**).
b. I'm sorry I can't talk now. I ..... (**help**) to make dinner.
c. On Saturday, we ..... (**get up**) quite early, usually at 8 o'clock.
d. My mother ..... (**work**) for the City Council. She's a lawyer.
e. Can't you see us? We ..... (**stand**) outside the ticket office.

EXPRESSING AGREEMENT AND DISAGREEMENT

4 **Say** if you agree with the following statements, and why.

a. School uniforms are a good idea.
b. Rap music is great.
c. Winter is the best time of year.
d. Black and blue clothes look really bad together.

NUMBERS

5 **Answer** the questions below. **Write** the numbers out in full.

a. How many days are there in December? ..... .
b. How many students are there in your English class today? ..... .
c. How many countries border France? ..... .
d. How many days are there in a year? ..... .

COLOURS

6 **Complete** the sentences below with the correct colours.

a. If you mix red and white you get ..... .
b. ..... and ..... are the colours of the Spanish flag.
c. Old photos and old films are in ..... and ..... .
d. The Moroccan flag has a ..... star.

CLOTHES

3 **Find** the odd one out in each list. **Justify** your answers.

a. shirt / shoes / trainers / socks

b. hoodie / skirt / dress / tights

c. bracelet / blazer / belt / beanie

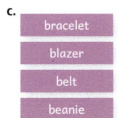
d. trousers / tie / blazer / flip-flops

Exercises

Unit 6 Let's play ball!

CAN / CAN'T AND ABILITY

1 Say if you play the following sports. Describe your level of ability.

2 Write the questions and answers to complete the dialogue.

a. Mr Jones: ......?
   James: Yes, I can. I ...... run very fast.

b. Mr Jones: ......?
   James: I ...... kick a ball quite well.

c. Mr Jones: ......?
   James: I'm very active and tough.

d. Mr Jones: ......?
   James: Yes, I am. I'm really skilful.

ADVERBS OF DEGREE

3 Complete this conversation using the correct adverbs.

Norah: What are your best subjects?
Helen: Well, I'm **really/a bit** good at physics, chemistry and technology. I always get more than a 9 out of 10.
Norah: Wow! Me, I'm not good at science subjects **at all/quite**. And I'm **at all/a bit** worried about the maths exam next week.
Helen: Well, maybe I can help you. I'm **quite/a bit** good at maths too. I want to study architecture at university and those subjects are **a bit/very** important.

NEED / NEED TO

4 Choose two sports and write the equipment and skills you need to play them.

LINKING WORDS

5 Complete the sentences below using and or but.

I am fit (1) ...... competitive, (2) ...... I am not skilful. I can run fast (3) ...... I can catch a ball quite well, (4) ...... I can't throw it at all.

My favourite food is fish (5) ...... chips. Well, I do like chips, (6) ...... not fish. So actually I prefer chicken (7) ...... chips.

SPORT AND EQUIPMENT

6 Read these rules and write the sport.

a. You must hit the ball with a bat: ......

b. To score points you must put the ball through the hoop: ......

c. Players must shoot the puck with the stick into the opposing team's net: ......

d. Players must throw stones down a sheet of ice. Each team must throw eight stones ......

ADJECTIVES THAT DESCRIBE CHARACTERISTICS

7 Are you very sporty? Use four adjectives below to describe yourself.

active clumsy fast slow
tough lazy skilful competitive

FOOD

8 Complete each label with the correct food.

a.   b.   c.   d.

Bloggers 1

Exercises

Unit 7 New York, New York

THE PAST SIMPLE OF TO BE

1 Complete the sentences with the past simple form of the verb to be.

a. I ..... in London two days ago.
b. We ..... happy to see him again.
c. She ..... sad to hear the news.
d. Yesterday the weather ..... really bad.
e. ..... she Maria's sister?

FORMING THE PAST SIMPLE

2 Place the verbs in the correct column.

REGULAR VERBS	IRREGULAR VERBS

3 Write sentences in the past simple, using the verbs from exercise 2.

4 Rewrite the phrases below in the past simple.

a. I go to school.
b. I have a good day.
c. She eats doughnuts everyday.
d. They spend a lot of money.

TIME MARKERS FOR THE PAST TENSE

5 Write sentences with the prompts.

before | ... week(s) ago | last week
in the past | in those days | in 2012

6 Complete the sentences below with the time markers in exercise 5.

a. ..... she came, I was ready to go.
b. Sally O'Connor came from Ireland to New York in 1924. She was very poor ..... .
c. I did my last exam ....., now I am on holiday.
d. They went to New York two ...., and they loved it.

PLACES IN A CITY

7 Complete the sentences below.

a. If I am ill, I go to the ..... .
b. If I want to eat, I sometimes go to a ..... .
c. If I want to go from one side of the river to the other, I take the ..... .
d. The boats are in the ..... .
e. If I want to see an art exhibition, I go to the ..... .

TRAVELLING AND EXPRESSING FEELINGS

8 Choose the correct answers.

When I **left/came/were** France for New York, I took a **boat/cold/river**. I **crossed/walked/drove** the ocean. I was ill and **lonely/difficult/rough**. But I was very **sick/happy/painful** to arrive in this country.

Unit 8 A trip to Scotland

WILL + VERB

1 You visit a fortune teller. Read her answers and write the questions.

a. You: .....?
The fortune-teller: No, you will live in a small village.

b. You: .....?
The fortune-teller: Yes, you will have an interesting job.

c. You: .....?
The fortune-teller: You will have three children.

d. You: .....?
The fortune-teller: Yes, you will be very happy.

2 Look at the picture and guess where Tom and Kate are going and what they will do during their holidays.

CONDITIONAL SENTENCES

3 Write four sentences that describe which activities you will do depending on the different weather conditions.

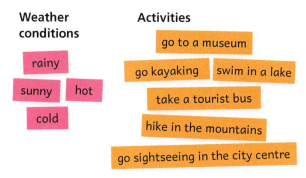

If it's rainy, I'll go to the museum.

TIME EXPRESSIONS

4 Write after, before or when.

Craig: Can I speak to Xavier, please? This is Craig.
Beth: He's not here at the moment.
Craig: Do you know ..... he'll be home?
Beth: At about 8 pm.
Craig: Hmm, I have to leave ..... 8. Can you ask him to phone me ..... 10 pm, please?
Beth: Sure. I'll give him your message ..... he gets home.

SUGGESTIONS

5 Your pen pal is in town this week. Suggest some places to visit and some activities to do.

THE WEATHER

6 Complete the sentences below with the help of the following words.

a. We can go skiing this weekend! There's a lot of ..... .
b. When there's a hurricane, you can expect extreme ..... .
c. It's not unusual in Britain and Ireland to have three or four ..... in one day.
d. Tomorrow will be a beautiful day – we can expect ..... weather.
e. You don't need to take your umbrella tomorrow because it won't ..... .

MEANS OF TRANSPORT

7 Answer the questions below with four different types of transport.

a. How do you go to school? ..... .
b. If you go to New York, how will you travel? ..... .
c. How do you go to the Isle of Skye? ..... .
d. You are an eco-tourist. How do you visit a city? (Give 2 possibilities.) ..... .

Unit 1 Reading

PUBLIC SCHOOL SUPERHERO
by James Patterson

Did you know?
James Patterson (1947*) is an American author known for his thrillers and his young adult fiction books.

Okay, in my neighborhood, my school is known as Fort Union. That's because of the crazy-strict military base rules there.

No kids get inside until 7:50 a.m., sharp.
5 No kids get inside without a student ID.
No kids get inside without opening their backpacks for the security guards.

And that's just the front door. I'm sure it'd take you less time to get through the airport's high-tech security
10 with explosives tied to your calves. It's crazy man. This is what I go through, every stinkin' day.

When I get past security, I find that my homeroom doesn't even have real windows. It's just metal screens where someone broke out the glass over the summer.

15 Also, it's kind of crowded in here. "Overcrowded" would be an understatement. For real.

After attendance, my homeroom teacher, Ms. Green, takes us around the school and shows us where everything is.

20 Downstairs on the first floor, the library's about the size of a closet. There's one rolling computer cart with two computers for the whole school.

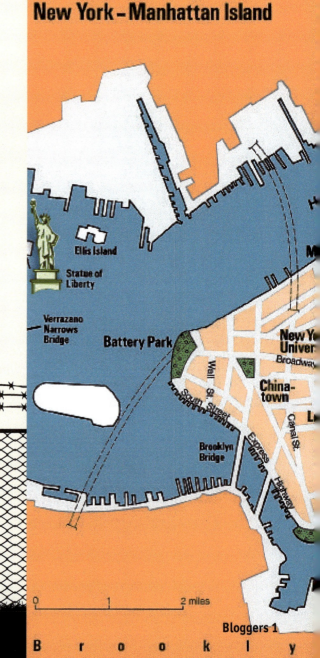

Unit 2 Reading

ESCAPE IN NEW YORK
Richard Musman

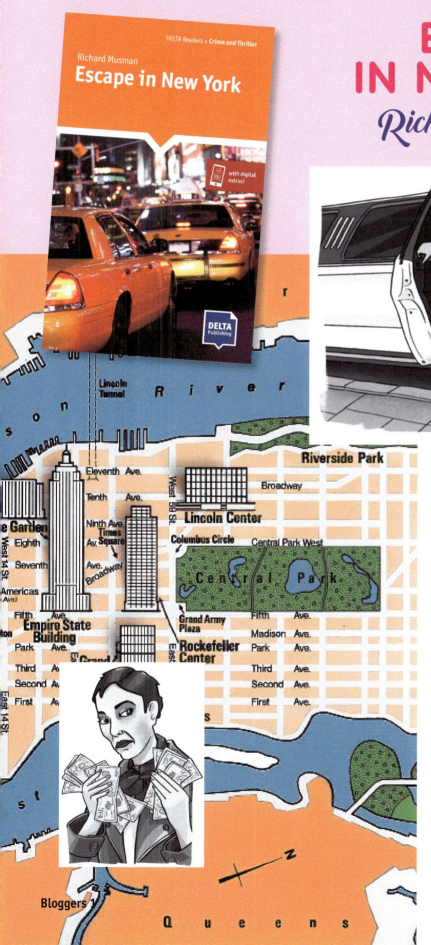

She sat down at her desk. Kevin admired his aunt and her enthusiasm. There were so many different ethnic groups in New York. There were
5 whole streets where Italians lived together. In fact, more Italians lived in New York than in Rome, more Jews than in Tel Aviv. There were the Irish Americans, who still called themselves
10 Irish and still hated the English.

He sat on the couch for a while, dreaming. The he fetched the telephone book which had names beginning with "O". He soon shut
15 the book. It was hopeless. There were hundreds of O'Briens. He shut the book with such a bang that Aunt Bella looked up from her desk.

"What's the matter, Kev? Who are you
20 looking for in that telephone book? A girlfriend?"

"Well, sort of."

Unit 3 Reading

The Story of Saint Patrick

James A. Janda

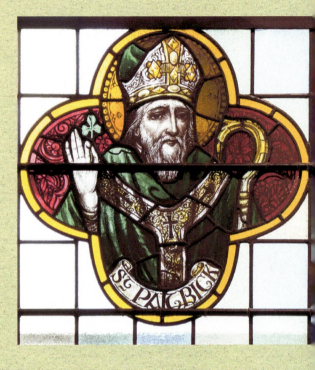

A little boy liked to sit on a hill and watch the boats come and go in and out of the harbor. His name was Patrick.

He liked to run down to the pier. He liked to watch the fishermen bring in their boats loaded with fish.

Patrick lived on the shore of England facing the Irish Sea. He wore a toga and sandals, because he was a citizen of Rome. He lived there a very long time ago —in the fifth century.

Patrick had to learn his prayers just as you and I. But, to tell the truth, young Patrick was more interested in playing than in learning. He liked to climb trees, pick apples, and play with his dog.

Patrick had a happy time until he turned sixteen. Then something happened that made him very sad.

From the top of the hill, he saw it all coming. Nial, the Celtic warrior, and his enemy boats were coming into the harbor.

Nial's warriors attacked the town. They killed many people. They burned the homes. They stole horses, pigs and sheep. They captured Patrick, forced him into a boat, and sailed across the sea to Ireland. In Ireland, Patrick was sold as a slave.

Did you know?
Saint Patrick is the patron saint of Ireland. Saint Patrick's Day is a very important celebration, held on 17th March.

Unit 4 Reading

If I Built a House
Chris Van Dusen

> **Did you know?**
> Chris Van Dusen (1960*) is an author and illustrator from Portland, Maine, in the US. He writes children's books.

Jack, in the backyard, said to his mother,

This house is OK, but it's like any other. It's boxy and boring and basically bland. It's nothing at all like the house I have planned.

5 My house will be different. It can't be the norm. I'll think about traffic flow, function, and form.

Oh, it may include shapes like a tower or dome, but I'll focus on what makes a building a home.

10 It's the rooms on the inside that make it unique, so step through the door and let's take a peek.

We'll start with the basics, right off the bat. Check out my new Kitchen-o-Mat!

You don't have to cook and you don't have
15 to clean, it's done by a space-age robotic machine.

It makes all the meals and the food is deeelish, then it washes and puts away every last dish.

The living room's next. It's fun! Come on in!
20 The chairs and the table and the sofa all spin!

And trampolines lead to a giant ball pit. It's a pretty neat room, you have to admit.

Unit 5 Reading

BACK TO SCHOOL SHOPPING
KENN NESBITT

My sleeves are too short
and my jeans are too tight.
My shirt is so small
that it doesn't fit right.

5 My hat is too snug
and my socks all have holes.
My shoes are worn out
on the sides and the soles.

My mom says it's time
10 to go shopping for more.
She wants me to get
some new clothes at the store.

She begs and cajoles,
but I simply say, "No.
15 I want to stay home.
I would rather not go."

While new ones may fit
in the sleeves and the toes,
the old ones I have
20 are my favorite clothes.

Did you know?
Ken Nesbitt (1962*) is an American children's author named Children's Poet Laureate by the Poetry Foundation.

Unit 6 Reading

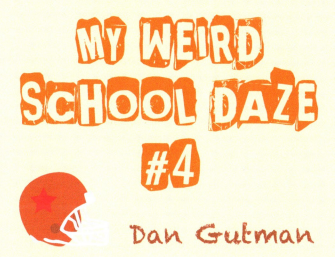

MY WEIRD SCHOOL DAZE #4

Dan Gutman

I love Pee Wee Football.

In the fall I play football every Saturday. Football is cool because you get to push and shove and yell and knock kids on their butts. And the best part is, you don't even get punished!

At school, if you push and shove and yell and knock kids on their butts, you have to go to the principal's office. But in football you're supposed to push and shove and yell and knock kids on their butts.

That's why I hate school and I love Pee Wee Football. If you ask me, the world would be a better place if they closed all the schools and turned them into Pee Wee Football camps.

The only problem is, my team stinks! We're called the Moose, and we lost every game last season. Every game!

The good news is, we're getting a new coach this year named Coach Hyatt. I bet he'll be a lot better than our old coach, Mr. Boozer. Mr. Boozer was a loser.

I put on my uniform and shoulder pads to get ready for our first practice. Shoulders pads are cool because they make it look like you have big muscles. Our uniform is red, and we have red helmets with a lightning bolt down the middle.

Did you know?
Dan Gutman (1955*) is an American writer, primarily of children's fiction, famous for his *My Weird School* series.

Unit 7 Reading

From New Amsterdam to the Big Apple
adapted from Richard Panchyk

Did you know?
Richard Panchyk is an American author, editor and translator from Queens, New York.

I often try to imagine what life was like for my great-great-grandfather, Carl Friedrich. He was the first of my ancestors to arrive in New York City. He got to Manhattan Island in 1866 as a young man of 18. There were people everywhere, endless streets and stone buildings. […]

Carl had little money. He took whatever job he could find, and he lived on the Lower East Side. There was only one shared bathroom and there were bugs and mice everywhere.

Carl worked hard. After some years, he became a US citizen, moved uptown to a better neighborhood, found a wife and started his business. […] Life wasn't easy. But he stayed and made it work.

Carl and millions of others like him are the people who made New York great. This is Carl's story. The story of New York.

Unit 8 Reading

Glasgow

William McGonagall

Beautiful city of Glasgow, with your streets so neat and clean,
Your stately mansions, and beautiful Green!
Likewise your beautiful bridges across the river Clyde,
And on your bonnie banks I would like to reside.

5 Then away to the West — to the beautiful West!
To the fair city of Glasgow that I like the best,
Where the river Clyde rolls on to the sea,
And the lark and the blackbird whistle with glee.

'Tis beautiful to see the ships passing to and fro,
10 Laden with goods for the high and the low;
So let the beautiful city of Glasgow flourish,
And may the inhabitants always find food their bodies to nourish.

And as for the statue of Sir Walter Scott that stands in George Square,
It is a handsome statue — few can with it compare,
15 And most elegant to be seen,
And close beside it stands the statue of Her Majesty the Queen.

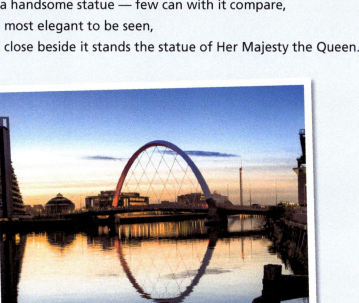

Did you know?
William McGonagall (1825-1902) was a Scottish poet. When he wrote this poem, Glasgow was an industrial desert.

How can I make sure I understand the instructions correctly?

Here are some tips to help you understand instructions.

1. Find the verb!
In the instructions, the verbs are the most important part.

It can help to create a mini notebook with instruction verbs. You can draw pictures to help you memorise the words.

Look at the "Instructions in your textbook" page at the beginning of this book for ideas.

Keep your mini notebook with your school books so you can look at it when you need!

2. Listen closely and ask if you don't understand!
It's normal if you don't understand everything. When you don't understand something, ask your teacher. You can ask when your classmates are doing a task if you're shy or embarassed.

Remember, if you don't understand, some of your classmates probably don't!

Drink a lot of water and sleep 8 hours per night to help you concentrate in class.

3. Think about it from another perspective
Think about the main objective.

Is there a project to do at the end of the school year?

If you understand the objective, you can organise the process!

NOW IT'S YOUR TURN!

1 Create a notebook with "instruction verbs"!

a. To start with, note down all the verbs below in your notebook. You can add more verbs when you find them.

b. Next to each verb, note down the meaning in your own language.
c. To finish off, think about illustrating each of the verbs!

How can you tell if something is true or false?

It's easy to believe new information. Sometimes it's just a person's opinion. How can you know? Here's how!

1. Stay alert!
Question sources of information. This includes texts, videos and the internet.

2. Who is providing the information? Investigate the author.
Imagine a car. The person selling the car says it's incredible. A person who worries about nature says a car is awful. They are talking about the same object! Think about the author's purpose.

3. Rephrase the information!
Repeat information and then say it with your own words. If can you, then you understand the information! Indicate where the information comes from.

4. Reflect and evaluate
You have understood. But can you tell the difference between opinion and fact? A fact is objective, it is the same for everyone. An opinion is subjective, it varies according to people's opinions. Is the information subjective or objective?

1. Beware of simplification!
Summarising a complex idea can be a good a task. But be careful! Simplifying means reducing and choosing the most important aspects, but it also means removing some information. This can encourage generalisations.

2. Think outside the box!
When you share these ideas, you are responsible for their consequences. Check that you really know about the topic. Be open to other people's opinions.

How does it work? The human brain likes logic, it tries to find immediate explanations. But reality can be complex. Some things are complicated to explain and that's fine!

The cat of the family

Can you believe the size of this cat?! Snowball is a monster! Snowball's mother (a normal-sized cat) was found near a nuclear laboratory. She later gave birth to Snowball, who weighed more than 40kg!

NOW IT'S YOUR TURN!

1. **Take a look** at the photo. What is your initial reaction?
2. After **reading** the text, how would you **explain** the size of the cat?
3. Think about it for a while. Where does the image come from? Where does the text come from?
4. Can you **verify** that it is true? One suggestion: **type** **"Snowball monster cat hoax"** in a search engine to check if it is **a hoax**.

How do I make a slide show presentation ?

> Spoken presentations can generate a lot of interest with your classmates! Follow these tips to give a great slide show presentation.

1. To prepare:
On paper, plan the information for each slide. Include one idea per slide.

On the slides:
Write max. 6 words per line.
Write max. 6 lines per slide.

2. Plan your presentation!
Open a new slide show and write these titles:
- the introduction: slide show topic + names of the authors + year made + a picture that matches the topic
- the titles and subtitles for the slides that follow,
- the conclusion slide: summary + conclusion + references / sources.

 How does it work? The brain likes receiving information that is categorised. Include categories in your slide show so your classmates understand!

3. Choose the right pictures!
Just because you find a picture on the internet doesn't mean you can use it! Use an image bank such as Pixabay, Freepik or FreeImages. Cite the author of the picture or the website where you found it.

4. Adapt your text
Your objective is to create a slide show that is easy to see and easy to read. It needs to be simple:
- Max. three main colours,
- use fonts arial, verdana or calibri, and make sure there is colour contrast (black on a light background),
- fonts in size 38 for titles and minimum size 24 for the text,
- use bullet points for lists. It makes the information clear.

 How does it work? Illustrations are important for a slide show. It is easier to remember an idea when it is associated with an image.

5. Add the finishing touches to your presentation
Add transitions and animations, but not too many or you will make your audience dizzy.

 How does it work? To understand and memorise information, the brain needs time and tranquillity. The brain needs clear information, lots details.

NOW IT'S YOUR TURN!

 1 In the **challenge** for Unit 3, you create a slide show about Tara's daily routine.
Do the activities on the worksheet.

Go further!
If you are comfortable with basic slide shows, you can create personal videos or presentations using online software like PowToon.

How can I memorise new information?

> Vocabulary, grammar rules, dates, ... Here are some tips to help you remember everything.

1. Participate in class

Listen, participate, highlight important information and copy the lesson with colours.

How does it work? In class, you use your "short-term memory". This part of your brain understands new things but it doesn't remember them.

2. Read out loud

When you are at home, close your textbook and write or say the words and expressions you have learned during class out loud.

3. Check

Read your textbook and note down anything you have forgotten in your rough workbook.

How does it work? Your brain forgets information that does not seem important. Look at your book. What things can you remember? Think about why.

4. Write

Read, re-read and write down any new words, expressions or phrases from your class. Use different colours to categorise new words.

How does it work? To remember something for a long period of time, your brain needs to make associations: a word with a colour, for example. Important information will then be stored in your "long-term memory".

5. Make flashcards

Make cards and draw pictures to illustrate new words. Write the new word on the back. Carry your cards around or play card games to practice your vocabulary.

6. Recite

Read new words out loud using the pronunciation guides in your coursebook. You can also film yourself, and watch the video back!

How does it work? When someone listens to you, your neurones work twice as hard!

NOW IT'S YOUR TURN!

1. Here is a list of some of the different counties in England. What categories can you **think of** to **classify** the names? Look your ideas.
   Which do you think is the best for memorising the names? **Compare** your answers with a classmate.

   Kent   Buckinghamshire   Dorset   West Sussex
   Surrey   Warwickshire   Derbyshire   Somerset
   Norfolk   East Sussex   Suffolk

2. **Memorise** the two first verses of the poem **Daisy the Snail** by following the tips on the worksheet provided by your teacher.

Go further!

Do you want a more difficult challenge? Memorise these eight cards in the right order. You can train yourself to memorise even more cards!

How can I use my notebook to work comfortably?

> If you write things down, it helps you. You can organise new information and remember it. Your notebook can help you!

1. Categorising your notes can improve your grade!

It's good to take notes... It's also important to be able to find your notes when you need them! To do this, you can:
- **Number the pages** of your notebook so you can find things quickly.
- **Note the date at the top** of the pages so you can see when you were studying each topic.
- **Colour in the page corners** in different colours depending on the topic, or **note the chapter number** at the bottom of each page.

2. How can I copy down the information I need?

- Copy words or phrases your teacher writes on the board. You can read the words by placing them in groups of 4 or 5 and repeating them in your head while copying them down.
- If you cannot read the board properly, **tell the teacher**.

> Excuse me, but I can't read this!

3. Words need to breathe!

Follow these tips to review new words:
- Write titles in the centre of the page and underline them.
- Leave a line empty or separate different topics by lines with **a ruler**.

4. Words: are they all the same?

In Year 6 you will learn many new words. To learn you can use different colours for groups of words. For example: nouns are blue, verbs are orange.

5. Personal expression? In the margin!

Use the margin to:
- **Highlight** interesting words.
- Note down the **translation** of words in your language.
- Note down a **synonym**, a **short definition**, a **word that summarises** the topic of a paragraph, a personal **illustration** or a **mnemonic expression**... anything you like!

6. Don't forget the decoration!

It is important to **illustrate and decorate** your notebook. It's a good way to enjoy your work.

NOW IT'S YOUR TURN!

1 **Create** a contents table for your English notebook!

a. **Number** the pages in your notebook and **take** a single sheet.

b. **Write** the page numbers, their title and their main topic on each line. You can also **copy** some of the most important words on the page.

c. When your contents table is complete, **stick it in** at the beginning or end of your notebook.
You can **check it** just before exams.

Go further!

There's nothing like a post-it! You can write down questions you want to ask in the next class. You can also note down information, definitions or an interesting fact to share with the class. What could you explain or ask in your next class? Write it on a post-it and stick it in your notebook!

How can I improve my writing when working as a team?

Do you need to produce written work? Team work is a great way to share ideas for your final assignment.

1. How do you divide tasks?
There are three essential elements for a group to work well:
Organisation (leading the group word), **ability** (the expertise of each member) and **atmosphere** (respect for each group member).
Some students enforce the rules. Others do specific tasks. Everyone shares information!

2. What steps do I need to follow?
a. Team work (5 min.):
The **group leader** will rephrase the instructions to make sure everyone understands. They can see who understands and can explain again if necessary.

b. Individual work (5 min.):
Each member of the group completes personal research outside the classroom and thinks about how to present the results to the group.

c. Team work (30 min.):
Guided by the **group leader**, the members of the group shares their information. The **timekeeper** controls the time. The **speech master** controls the volume!

The **expert** chooses the best ideas. One student writes down the key words.

The **referee** makes sure the group members interact well with each other: listening to each other, finding agreements when group members give different opinions, and making sure everyone is polite.

d. Individual work (10 min.):
Each group member notes down the result of the discussion in their notebook. You can use the **expert**'s notes.

Everyone has everything they need to complete the written task!

NOW IT'S YOUR TURN!

1. The **challenge** in Unit 6 is to **create** a **poster** about an American sport (p. 93).
To create the poster, there are three jobs: an artist to illustrate the poster, a writer to write the text and a computer expert to find useful websites.
Which of these roles would you like? Why?

2. The **challenge** in Unit 1 involves creating a **yearbook** for your class (p. 29).
Imagine that you are working in groups of 5.
   a. **Write a list** of the 5 roles you need to complete the challenge.
   b. **Choose** one of these roles and **explain** why.

Go further!
The American Howard Gardner described eight forms of intelligence. Of these, interpersonal intelligence is the type of intelligence that allows us to guess the intentions and feelings of others, and to interact with them in an appropriate way. In your class, who do you think has the most interpersonal intelligence? What does this person do to get the group to understand each other and to resolve any conflicts?

How can I improve my cultural knowledge?

> You will learn about different parts of the world/ For example: Ireland, Scotland and the United States. You can learn about different cultures!

1. Find out more!
Unit 7 includes tourist sites, food and architecture in New York. You can choose a topic and find out more about it.

If you like sport, search for "sports in New York" on the internet.

2. Work on your memory!
When you find information on the internet, test your memory. Read it out loud or write it down. Then the information stays in your brain!

3. Share with others!
In the **Culture Blog** in Unit 7, **You are an artist** you research famous buildings in New York and make a poster to compare their sizes. Exchange information with your classmates! This will help you memorise the information.

4. Take an interest in current affairs!
You have lots of sources of information: newspapers, podcasts, TV programmes and websites.

Access the news in English. You will learn about the world and improve your English!

5. Read magazines!
Have a look in your school library for magazines in English for your age group and level of English.

You can make flash cards to help you remember the articles you have read. Note down any new vocabulary you have learned.

6. Watch cartoons in their original language!
Watch cartoons in their original language to help you improve your English skills. You can put on subtitles in English to help you understand.

You will also learn about the culture. For example, if you are working on unit 7, watch **The Secret Life of Pets**. It's set in Manhattan!

NOW IT'S YOUR TURN!

1. Do you want to speak perfect English? **Ask** your teacher for a list of websites to look at. This will allow you to practice in a fun way, while improving your pronunciation and reading skills while learning about English-speaking countries.

How can I understand an audio?

> Understanding a listening exercise is like a puzzle: you need to put the pieces together so that they make sense. Here's how.

1. Think positive!
If your teacher plays you a listening exercise, it will be related to the chapter you are studying. This means you can be sure that you will find information you already know. Be confident in your abilities!

2. Be ready to listen!
Your teacher will suggest one or two pre-listening activities that will prepare you. For example, a picture can help you to think about the words in the listening exercise.

3. Listen to understand the context
Listen to the exercise without taking notes.
- Listen for all the audio cues (music, background noise, etc.) to imagine the scene.
- Pay attention to the voices (are they children? men? women?) to identify the people and their names.

These clues will help you decide what kind of recording it is: a film, radio show, weather report, news report, interview.

4. Listen to the keywords
Listen again and write down the important words. These are the key words.

Write down names and numbers.

Don't write down grammatical words. For example: a / the.

If you're working in a group, share your words!

How does it work? Your brain cannot process and categorise all of this information at the same time. Notes can help you concentrate, understand and remember.

5. Listen to the emotions
Listen to the intonation and tone of voice: the tone indicates emotions. You can hear if people are angry, disappointed or happy.

NOW IT'S YOUR TURN!

Track: 15

1. You will listen to an audio. To prepare, look at the picture and make a list of words to describe it.

2. Listen to the recording. Try closing your eyes to help you focus. What is the name of the person speaking? Who is talking? What can you understand about what kind of recording it is?

3. Listen again. Choose the keywords from the words and expressions below.

Go further!
You can practice alone and make progress outside of your English classes. Always watch your favourite TV shows or films in the original version, to help train your ears. Check the examples on the website http://www.elllo.org, which has a number of listening activities at a "beginner" level.

How to have a telephone conversation

It's easy to talk on the phone. But it's difficult in another language! Don't panic: with these tips, you will soon be able to call anyone you want!

1. Here are some expressions you can use to say the right thing in every situation:

• At the start of a conversation…

> Hello! This is Enzo. I'd like to speak with Mia/Oliver, please.

> Hello? Yes, this is Mia / Oliver speaking.

• If you need to think about it…

> Let me see…

> Let me think…

> Er… Well…

• If you haven't understood the caller…

> I'm sorry, I don't understand.

> I'm not English. Can you speak slowly?

> Can you repeat, please?

> So, you said, '…', right?

• Before ending the call…

> All right. Thank you and goodbye!

> You're welcome. Have a nice day!

2. If the person you are calling doesn't answer the phone, leave a message:

• Introduce yourself:

> Hello, this is Enzo.

• Give the reason for your call

> I would like to invite Mandy to my party.

• Leave your telephone number:

> Call me back on 33 1 23 61 45 67.

• Say goodbye before hanging up:

> Thank you! Goodbye!

3. Don't forget:

• Speak clearly and put the right intonation in your sentences. Just because you can't see the other person, it doesn't mean that you have to stay still. You can understand everything over the phone, even a smile!

 NOW, LET'S CALL!

The telephone labyrinth
Stand back to back with a classmate. One of you starts the call and **chooses** a conversation starter.
Take it in turns to start the call.
Try to speak for 30 seconds, then 1 minute!

How to understand a text

Oh no... your teacher has given you a text to read and you panic. You think you don't understand it. Take a deep breath a follow these tips. You'll get there!

1. Look around!

• The texts in your manual are often accompanied by illustrations and a title on the same topic. **Use what you can see** to identify the general topic of the text.

2. Look inside!

• Even if you don't understand everything, **you can still identify some elements of the text**:

- **Names** (people and places) always start with a capital letter.

- **Subject pronouns** (I, you, him, us, etc.) provide information about the characters.

- **Dates** indicate the time period in question.

• If possible, **underline** these elements in different colours. Otherwise, take notes. This will allow you to answer these questions: **WHO? WHERE? WHEN?**

• Linking words **and** and **but** can help you understand a sentence.

- **and** adds a similar idea: My sister has black **and** big trousers. → You can understand that this is another detail about his trousers.

- **but** introduces an opposing idea: I enjoy baseball **but** not lacrosse. → Baseball is a sport, so there is a high chance that lacrosse is also a sport.

• **Even if you are missing a piece in a jigsaw puzzle, you can still see the final picture.** The same thing happens with a text!
What do you think jewellery means?

There is a beautiful necklace in this jewellery shop!

• **Try drawing** some elements of the text to better visualise them.

3. Look again!

• Some English words can be similar to words in other languages. If you see a word similar to a word in your language, see if it makes sense.

hello / hola / óla / hallo

4. Look for more!

• When you have a text to read at home, **check the meaning of words in your dictionary.** Create your own personal vocabulary list.

• **Practice your reading** with the Reading sections of your manual!

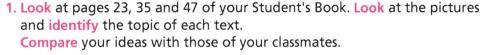

NOW, LET'S START READING!

1. **Look** at pages 23, 35 and 47 of your Student's Book. **Look** at the pictures and **identify** the topic of each text.
   Compare your ideas with those of your classmates.

2. **Read** the text that your teacher gives you and **answer** the questions, using the tips given on this page.

How to improve your written work

Short sentences are fine. Rich sentences are better! Here are some tips to help you get closer to the level of an English-speaker of the same age!

1. Work on details!

• Readers are always curious. **They love more information!**

My sister is 15. → very short!

My sister is 15. She has long hair. She has two hamsters, and she loves skateboarding. → Much more interesting!

• Add adjectives to make your descriptions more visual!

My sister has long hair. → My **big** sister has **long brown wavy** hair.

> To remember the order of adjectives in a sentence, think about a **TACO**!
>
> **T**allness (big, small)
> **A**ge (old, young)
> **C**olour (blue, red)
> **O**rigin (American, French)

• Use different verbs so you don't repeat the same ones.

I like pancakes. → I **love** pancakes.

I like sports. → I **enjoy** sports.

I don't like spiders. → I **hate** spiders!

• Does what you are talking about happen often, rarely, or never? **Use adverbs of frequency** (usually, often, always, never). Remember to use them **before the verb**.

I eat breakfast at 7 o'clock. → I **always** eat breakfast at 7 o'clock.

2. Work on logic!

• What is the secret to a well-written text? **Linking words** (like but, and, because)! Use them to make your ideas and event clear.

This is my new school. This is my classroom. I like it. It is comfortable.
→ This is my new school, **and** this is my classroom. I like it **because** it is comfortable.

• If your story is chronological, use **time expressions** (First…, Then…, Afterwards…) to better explain the different stages in the story.

I have mathematics. I go to history class. It is time for a break.
→ **First**, I have mathematics. **Then**, I go to history class. **Afterwards**, it is time for a break.

NOW, LET'S CAPTIVATE THE READER!

1. **Make** these sentences **more interesting** by adding as many adjectives as possible.
   a. My pet is a dog. b. I like cake. c. My friend is a girl.

2. Tom has the same routine every morning. **Write** the most interesting paragraph possible to explain his routine, using the words given by your teacher. Don't forget **to use** time expressions and adverbs of frequency.

3. **Write** a single sentence with a linking word.
   a. I have a brother. I have two sisters.
   b. I love this sweater. It is a beautiful colour.
   c. My house is big. We have a small garden.

4. Longest sentence contest! **Follow** the instructions given by your teacher.

How to make a poster

A poster is the perfect way to give a message to many people at the same time. Here are some key points for creating perfect posters!

1. Make it visual!

Title: Short and written in bold so it can be seen from far away. The title presents the subject of the poster in a lively and eye-catching way.

Layout: Make sure to leave enough space on the **page**.

Subtitle: A short sentence **that gives more details about** the subject of the poster.

Picture(s): One or several colour pictures that fit with the topic and are big.

Format: Use **a large sheet of paper**, so your poster is easy to see.

2. Make it interesting!

• The **title** is the **main feature** of your poster as it attracts attention and explains the topic. It should be **short and catchy**. To do this, you can: repeat the same word, repeat the same sound, ask a question, use an exclamation.

• **Subtitles** provide **more information on the topic** of the poster. It tells the reader to do something. For example, you can:

– use an action verb in the imperative: discover..., learn..., watch..., come...

– use the imperative in the negative form: don't do this!

NOW, LET'S BE CREATIVE!

1. **Use** one of these techniques for each title.

   a. WHAT'S YOUR TALENT?
   b. COOL SCHOOL
   c. SPORTS, SPORTS, SPORTS!
   d. LET'S GO!

   1. A repeated word
   2. A repeated sound
   3. Question
   4. Exclamation

2. With a classmate, imagine the title and subtitle for three posters that your teacher has given you.

How to write an email or a letter

You are lucky, you have found an English-speaking pen pal! To get to know each other and start a discussion by letter or by email, use the examples below for help!

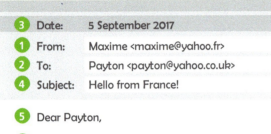

Email:

- ③ Date: 5 September 2017
- ① From: Maxime <maxime@yahoo.fr>
- ② To: Payton <payton@yahoo.co.uk>
- ④ Subject: Hello from France!

⑤ Dear Payton,

⑥ My name is Maxime and I am your new penfriend.

⑦ I am 11 years old. I live in a nice house in Pornic and I have two big brothers and a dog.

⑧ What about you? Tell me about your family.

⑨ See you soon!

⑩ Maxime

Letter:

① Maxime Dupuis
2 rue de l'océan
44 210 Pornic
FRANCE

② Joe Haley
230 South Peck Dr
Beverly Hills, CA, 90
USA

③ 26 December 2017

⑤ Dear Uncle Joe,

⑥ Thank you for the Christmas present. It's beautiful and I love it!

⑦ I am sending you a picture of the family!

⑧ When are you coming to France?

⑨ Love,

⑩ Maxime

1. Sender (the person who sends the letter)
2. Recipient (the person who receives the letter)
3. Date
4. Email subject
5. Opening the letter
6. Objective of the letter (to introduce yourself, send a thank you)
7. Explanation and details
8. Introducing another topic
9. Closing the letter
10. Signature

• **Choose the greeting you use** depending on the person you are writing to!

RECIPIENT	OPENING THE LETTER	CLOSING THE LETTER
Family or friends	• Dear Uncle Joe • My dear Mitchell	• See you soon! • Hugs and kisses! • XXX (kisses) • Love
Someone you don't know	• Dear Mr Hurley • Dear Mrs Lawrence	• Best regards • Yours

NOW, LET'S GET WRITING!

1. **Write** the following letters. They should include all the necessary information but be very short (two sentences maximum).
   a. An email to your cousin in New York to thank her for the postcard from Los Angeles
   b. A letter from your pen pal in London talking about your favourite sport
   c. A letter to Mr. McRae from the tourist office in Glasgow to tell him you would like a map of the city

How to prepare for and act out a scene

Do you have to act out a scene in English with a classmate? Don't panic! Use these tips to impress the audience!

1. Get into character!

- **Read the instructions properly** to find out:
  - **who your character is:** an English student, a journalist, or an animal?
  - **who you are writing to:** a friend, a salesperson, or a teacher?
  - **where you are:** in a shop, in a house, or in a tourist agency?
  - **your objective:** to get information or to organise a trip?

- If you need more information, **imagine what you need** so you can visualise the scene. To help you, **fill in the table** below. To make it more realistic **use props** and **create a set!**

Name: Alex
Age: 12
Job: pupil
Personality: shy, friendly
Feelings at the moment of the conversation: hungry
Place of the conversation: school cafeteria
Goal of the conversation: have information on the school menu
Who the character is speaking to: the cook

2. Get ready!

- The scene should look natural. Imagine what you would say in a certain situation and **note down any vocabulary and expressions that will be useful.** Don't write down everything and **don't memorise everything**!
For a scene in the canteen, you could note down the following, for example:

– **Vocabulary:** food / meal / dessert / fruit...
– **Expressions:** I'd like... / Can you...?

3. Be natural!

- Don't forget to greet the other person at the start and say goodbye at the end!

- A conversation is more than just words! Think about **your tone of voice** happy or angry. **Hand gestures** and even **imitating** your partner!

  NOW, LET'S PLAY!

Track: 16

1. This sentence is recorded with a different intonation every time. **Listen** and **identify** the person's emotion.

   My name is Cameron.   happy   sad   shy   angry

2. In groups of 2 or 3 people: every person should **choose** an emotion. Then **say** the sentence in exercise 1 with that tone of voice. The others guess the emotion. Then **repeat** with your own sentences. Who is the best actor?

How to give a talk or a speech

Does speaking in public make you nervous? Don't panic! Follow these tips and take a deep breath. You'll see that it's not too difficult!

1. Understand the job!

• First of all, **carefully read the instructions** given by your teacher:

- **What** will you be talking about (your family, school, hobbies, etc)?
- **Who** will you be talking to (your classmates, your English pen pal, a group of tourists, etc)?
- What is your **objective** (to explain, present, convince, etc)?
- Are there any **guidelines** to follow (comment on pictures, make a video, use a certain tense, etc)?

NOW, YOU'RE ON!

1. **Place** these sentences in the correct order to **create** a structured talk.
   a. Second, I don't like sports. I am terrible at basket-ball.
   b. Today, my presentation is about... me!
   c. My name is Nora and I am French.
   d. Finally, my favourite subject at school is History.
   e. First, I love movies! My favourite movie is **Hunger Games**.
   f. Good afternoon everyone!
   g. That is all. Thank you and goodbye!

2. Organise yourself!

• So that your audience can follow your thoughts, **make sure to structure your speech** in several parts:

- **1.** Welcome and introduction to the topic,

> My subject is sports.

> Hello everyone! Today, my presentation is about my family.

> I want to talk about New York City.

- **2.** Presenting the different ideas to be covered, in order,

> First, ... Secondly, ... Thirdly, ... Finally, ...

- **3.** Conclusion and goodbye.

> That's all. Thank you and goodbye.

• When preparing your speech, **don't write everything down**! Only write down the **main ideas** for each one of the parties.

3. Use keywords!

• **Only memorise the keywords**: the most important words in your presentation so your audience can understand your speech. These words should be **emphasised in spoken English**.

For example, in the sentence *Music is very important for me*, the keywords are *music* and *important*.

• If you can't remember what to say, **use short words like** *er...* or *well...* while you find your place again.

NOW, YOU'RE ON!

2. **Note down** the keywords in this extract from a talk.

> In the morning, I wake up at 7 o'clock. I always take a shower before breakfast. I take the bus to school on Monday and Tuesday. I don't take the bus on Wednesday.

Track: 17

3. Now, **listen** to the talk. **Identify** the words that the person stresses. This will help you confirm that you found the right keywords.

4. Using the same keywords as in the previous exercises, **give** your own speech.

4. It's a question of attitude!

• Even if you are not comfortable with public speaking, **act like you are**!

– **Look at your classmates.** Look at some of your friends in class to give you courage.

– **Talk loudly, slowly and clearly** so that everyone can understand you.

– **Stand up straight and use hand gestures and facial expressions** to illustrate what you are saying.

– **Feel free to move** around the room and, if you are using pictures during your talk, **point out** the things you are talking about to your classmates.

• When preparing for the talk, **practise in front of a mirror** and/or with your family.

NOW, YOU'RE ON!

5. To help improve your self-confidence, **play** the game **Truth or Lie?** with your classmates. Each person should **give information** (true or false) with the most confidence possible. The goal is to **make the others believe** the most ridiculous things!

5. Shakespeare, my dear!

• To make sure you are understood, you must **pronounce things correctly**! Always learn new words **by listening to and repeating their pronunciation**.

• **Think about sentence stress.**
Remember: when a word ends in a consonant and the next word starts with a vowel, **the two words should be pronounced like one word**.
On the other hand, when a word ends in a letter and the next word starts with the same letter, **the repeated letter is only pronounced once**.

NOW, YOU'RE ON!

6. **Say** these sentences with the correct stress.
   a. I'm the king of the world! **(Titanic)**
   b. Winter is coming! **(Game of Thrones)**
   c. I don't want to forget. **(Finding Dory)**

7. **Say** the phrases below:
   a. This is a pretty bedroom!
   b. What time is it?
   c. I hate ants.
   d. She's eating a banana.
   e. I need a new coat.

   When listening to you talk, we should know whether your are enthusiastic, angry, happy. **Express your emotions** by using the correct intonation!

How to read over your homework

Did you finish your English homework? Make sure everything is correct by checking over the following points before handing your homework to your teacher!

1. Everything in its place!

• A simple sentence is: a subject, a verb and, often, an object. Don't forget anything!

I	like	chocolate.
subject	verb	object

My mother	loves	cakes.
subject	verb	object

• Adjectives (words that describe a noun) are placed **before** nouns.

a	blue	car
	adj.	noun

2. Let's agree

• **In the simple present tense, verbs have an -s at the end in the third person singular** (he, she, Tom...).

I play basketball. Jason plays tennis.

• **All modal verbs are used in the same way:** can / must + verb root (= verb in the infinitive without **to** and without **-ing**).

They **must** work. She **can** be very funny.

• **Adjectives never have an -s at the end in their plural form in English.**

My best friends are Emily and Pam.

• **Use the article** an **and not** a **in front of words that start with a vowel**, to make pronunciation easier: an aunt, an arm...

3. Pay attention to the details!

• Take a few minutes to make sure your **punctuation and spelling are correct**!

• Remember that **some nouns are always written with a capital letter**: **countries** and their **inhabitants**, **languages**, **nationalities**, **days** of the week and **months**.

4. Don't confuse them!

• there **is** + singular
  there **are** + plural

If you know you need to count, you have to use there are.

• Pay attention so **you don't get confused**:
– you're (you are) / your:
You're my friend. ≠ Your pen is on the table.

– they're (they are) / their / there:
They're sad. ≠ Their life is great. ≠ Look over there!

– it's (it is) / its:
I love your house: it's very pretty! ≠ I like its style.

NOW, LET'S REVISE!

1. These sentences were written by an absent-minded student. **Correct them**!
   a. I love chocolate! What is you're favourite food?
   b. I doesn't think its true.
   c. My best friend have eyes blues.
   d. There is three books english on the table.
   e. New York? Its a amazing city!

TIP

Every time your teacher gives you back a homework task, **look** at the mistakes you made and **note them down** in a workbook or on a sheet of paper. Before your next homework, **re-read** them to avoid making the same mistakes!

CULTURE IN SOUNDS

Track: 18

English vowels

a bl**a**ck c**a**b /æ/   a sm**ar**t gu**ar**d /ɑ:/   a delic**a**te eleph**a**nt /ə/   a p**ur**ple p**ur**se /ɜ:/   a r**e**d dr**e**ss /e/

a gr**ee**n qu**ee**n /i:/   a p**i**nk k**i**lt /ɪ/   a sm**a**ll d**oo**r /ɔ:/   an **o**dd bulld**o**g /ɒ/   a bl**ue** m**oo**n /u:/

a g**oo**d b**oo**k /ʊ/   a f**u**nny b**u**s /ʌ/   a gr**ey** cupc**a**ke /eɪ/   a n**oi**sy paperb**oy** /ɔɪ/   wh**i**te ch**i**na /aɪ/

a br**ow**n cr**ow**n /aʊ/   a r**a**re teddy b**ea**r /eə/   a p**u**re t**ou**rist /ʊə/   a yell**ow** rainc**oa**t /əʊ/   a sev**e**re d**ee**r /ɪə/

Track: 19

English consonants

Engli**sh sh**oes /ʃ/   a **Ch**inese **ch**air /tʃ/   orange **j**am /dʒ/   a wor**th**y fa**th**er /ð/

three **th**ieves /θ/   a **h**ot bowler **h**at /h/   a lovi**ng** so**ng** /ŋ/

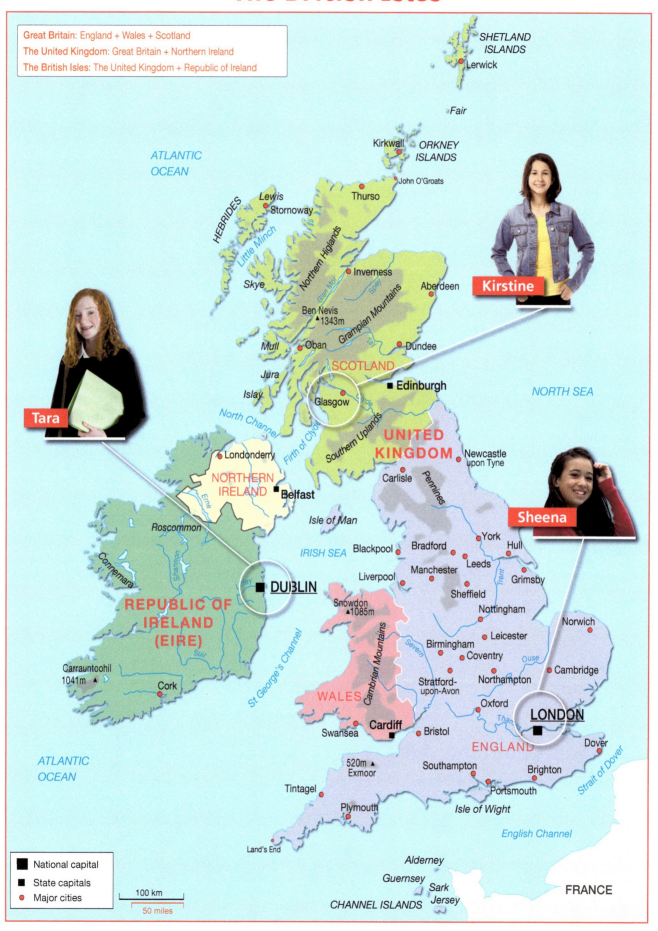

The United States of America

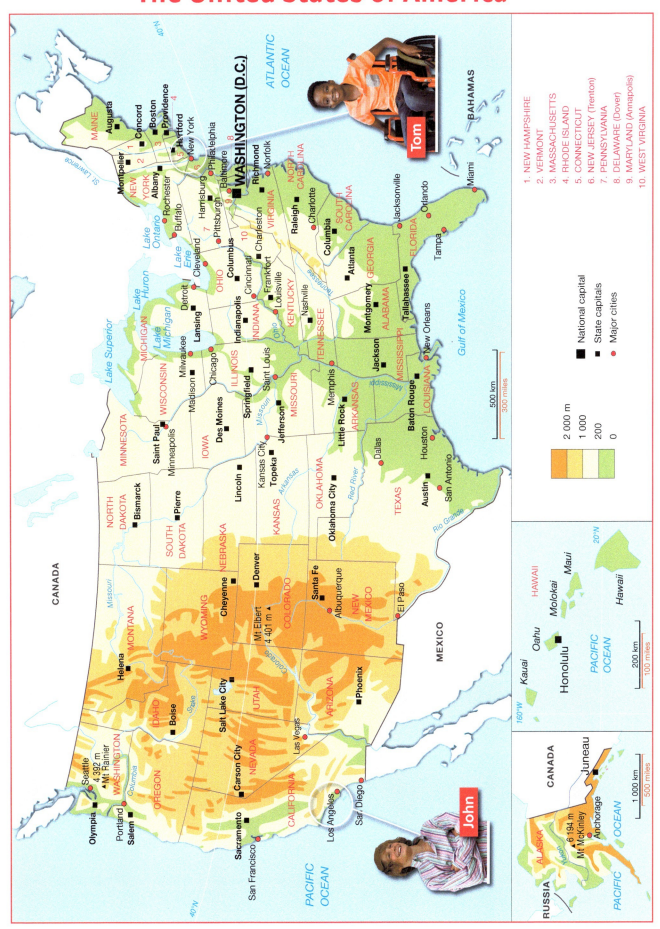

The English-speaking world

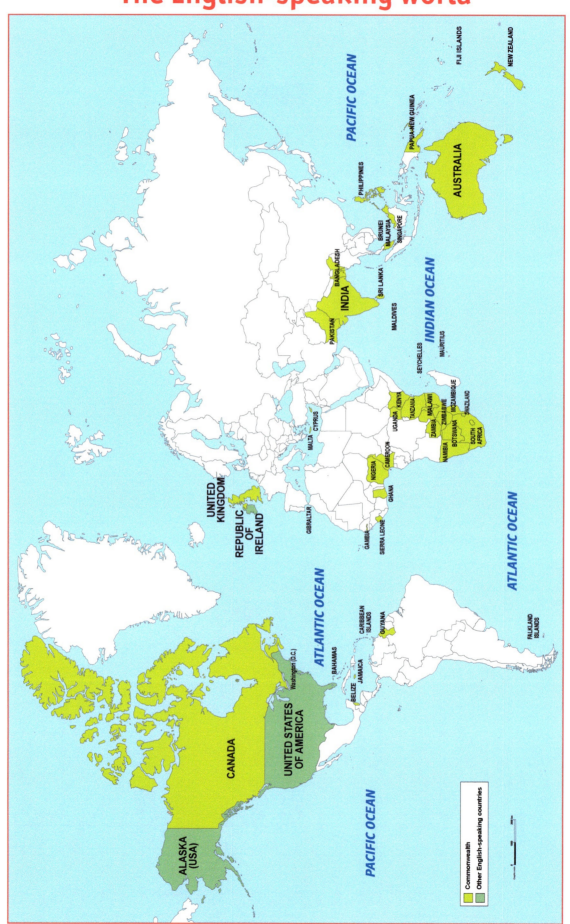

Acknowledgements

Images

123RF.com, Nidderau: **13** (Andriy Popov); **13** (ruslankphoto); **21** (kornienko); **28** (stockillustration); **29** (Shvadchak Vasyl); **33** (bloodua); **41** (damedeeso); **64** (buzzfuss); **65** (sudowoodo); **68, 147** (123rfaurinko); **68** (Elnur Amikishiyev); **68** (Evgeny Tomeev); **68** (Natalia Nazarenko); **68** (Pramual Jermjun); **68** (Ron Sumners); **68** (Sviatlana Shpak); **68** (avesun); **68** (monika3stepsahead); **68** (stocksnapper); **69** (Ineta Alvarado); **69** (Volodymyr Melnyk); **69** (sugarwarrior); **70** (Andreja Donko); **70** (Maria Mitrofanova); **70** (Nataliya Korolevskaya); **70** (PAUL HAKIMATA); **70** (Sebastian Radu); **70** (Xiaodong Sun); **71** (wrangel); **72** (Dmitry Naumov); **72** (Sommai Damrongpanich); **72** (evaletova); **72, 147** (tarzhanova); **73** (Tatiana Gladskikh); **73** (Vlad Teodor); **73** (satina); **73** (tupungato); **75** (PHOKIN WHANSAD); **75** (vectomart); **77** (Sylvie Bouchard); **82** (Arunas Gabalis); **82** (Denis Pepin); **82** (ronniechua); **84** (sergeypykhonin); **86** (Bradford Calkins); **89** (Volker Schlichting); **89** (habrda); **93** (myvector); **94** (ssviluppo); **95** (greatandlittle); **98** (merfin); **98** (microone); **99** (Dmitrii Starkov); **100** (sborisov); **101** (maglara); **101** (maximkabb); **104** (cougarsan); **113** (maszas); **115** (kzenon); **117** (Anna Yakimova); **119** (M.G. Mooij); **119** (winterstorm); **138** (alexutemov); **139** (Noppadol Anaporn); **141** (Maxim Popov); **142** (Dragana Eric); **142** (Pavel Ignatov); **145** (Kostiantyn Rassylnov); **145, 145** (iimages); **146** (Mahmud Fajar Rosyadi); **147** (Beata Predko); **147, 147** (Eric Isselee); **147** (Hanna Macharidis); **147** (John McAllister); **147** (Kamil Cwiklewski); **147** (Prapan Ngawkeaw); **147** (Sergey Sukhorukov); **147** (Somchai Somsanitangkul); **147** (Tatyana Tomsickova); **147** (VITALII SHCHERBYNA); **147** (Valentyna Chukhlyebova); **147** (W.Scott McGill); **147** (blueringmedia); **147** (maridav); **147, 147** (nerthuz); **147** (serezniy); akg-images, Berlin: **95** (Fototeca Gilardi); Alamy, Abingdon, UK: **129** (GL Archive); CartoonStock.com, Bath: **59** (Madden, Chris); **69** (Beyl, Charles); Chaney Farrell Academy of Irish Dance, Dublin: **46**; gemeinfrei **35**; Getty Images, München: **5** (blackwaterimages); **7** (Matt84); **7** (Wavebreakmedia); **7** (batuhanozdel); **7** (funduck); **12** (ozgurdonmaz); **16** (wundervisuals); **17** (golero); **17** (leminuit); **17** (lolaira); **17** (qingwa); **20** (JohnnyGreig); **23** (DragonFly); **23** (bandian1122); **29** (Robert Nicholas); **35** (FrankRamspott); **36, 37** (Juanmonino); **37** (DGLimages); **41** (ferrantraite); **53** (adventtr); **59** (4x6); **65** (3DMAVR); **68** (SolStock); **69** (Ben Pipe Photography); **83** (Mike Powell); **88** (cmannphoto); **Cover** (Donald Miralle); **Cover** (Shelly Allen Art); **88** (terryjack); **94** (Edwin Levick); **95** (Lewis W. Hine); **112** (georgeclerk); **129** (theasis); **130** (nadia_bormotova); **131** (Igor Zakowski); **137** (ntzolov); **139** (InnaBodrova); **141** (SDI Productions); **143** (alashi); **143** (rendixalextian); **145** (Visual Generation); **147** (bobey100); **147** (selimaksan); **Cover** (track5); Illustration by Josh Hurley **70**; Jeffrey Beall (licensed under Creative Commons Attribution 3.0 Unported license) **126**; Klett-Archiv, Stuttgart: **1** (Laura Broadbent); **122, 123** (G. Wustmann) **123** (Grit Döhnel); Look and Learn **112**; Marks and Spencer **77**; mauritius images, Mittenwald: **40** (Pictorial Press Ltd / Alamy); Penguin Random House LLC **125**; Printed by permission of the Norman Rockwell Family Agency © 1943 (Freedom From Want) the Norman Rockwell Family Entities **40**; Printed by permission of the Norman Rockwell Family Agency ©1947 (Going and Coming) the Norman Rockwell Family Entities **32**; Richard Panchyk **128**; Scott Garrett **107**; Shutterstock, New York: **Cover** (Africa Studio); **Cover** (Aitor Bouzo Ateca); **3, 19, Cover** (Galina Barskaya); **5** (Luria); **5, 64** (Tntk); **7** (Andrey Yurlov); **7, Cover, 79** (Simone van den Berg); **12** (Kamira); **12** (Michael Kaercher); **13** (Emma_ Griffiths); **13** (Madrugada Verde); **16** (Alfaenergy); **16** (Bikeworldtravel); **16** (ComposedPix); **16** (Hasanov Jeyhun); **16** (Ian Francis); **16** (Milleflore Images); **16** (Umomos); **16** (Zmiter); **16** (michal812); **16** (photastic); **17** (JASPERIMAGE); **17, 65** (Rawpixel.com); **17** (Smileus); **17** (Stephen Coburn); **17** (StockImageFactory.com); **17** (kurhan); **17** (kuvona); **17** (rozbyshaka); **19** (4691); **19** (Katerina Davidenko); **20** (M.Stasy); **20** (ajt); **20** (jackhollingsworth. com); **21** (Evgeniy_D); **21, 69** (Jacek Chabraszewski); **21** (dimair); **22** (Lemonade Serenade); **23** (ONYXprj); **24** (dikobraziy); **25** (ChetnaC); **25** (SergiyN); **25** (linear_design); **28, 76** (Featureflash Photo Agency); **28** (Ronald Sumners); **28** (solomon7); **29** (SvetaVector); **29** (Tracy Whiteside); **30** (wassiliy-architect); **31** (Kudryashka); **31** (Michael Zech Fotografie); **31** (View Apart); **32** (MeSamong); **33** (Padma Sanjaya); **33, 43, 44** (lineartestpilot); **33** (strekalova); **34** (miumi); **37, 53** (Visual Generation); **39** (Monkey Business Images); **39, Cover, 81** (wavebreakmedia); **40** (Somchai kong); **41** (DenisNata); **41** (Just dance); **41** (Minerva Studio); **42** (MichaelJayBerlin); **43, 98** (Art studio G); **43** (StockSmartStart); **43** (Suradech Prapairat); **44** (Helha); **44** (Mega Pixel); **44** (PchelaMajka); **45** (Leah-Anne Thompson); **45** (Viktoria Kazakova); **46** (Alfa Photostudio); **46** (Azurhino); **46, 52** (David Spieth); **46** (Monkey Business Images); **46** (spaxiax); **47** (2xSamara.com); **47** (d3verro); **51** (Axel Wolf); **51** (David Gilder); **51** (James Clarke); **51** (Jit-anong Sae-ung); **51** (Maglara); **51** (Michal Dzierzynski); **51** (Telnov Oleksii); **52** (Aurelien CURTET); **52** (Rus S); **52** (jjmtphotography); **52** (outsideclick); **52** (shellyallenart); **53** (bluedog studio); **53** (clearviewstock); **54** (Gabriele Maltinti); **55** (Les Perysty); **55** (Photographee.eu); **56** (Susse_n); **56** (VitaminCo); **57** (Cocos.Bounty); **58** (Emese); **58** (Lorelyn Medina); **58** (MJTH); **Cover** (Joshua Haviv); **Cover** (Richie Chan); **58** (Olesia Bilkei); **58** (Prostock-studio); **59** (3D Vector); **59** (Alexandra_F); **59** (Happy Art); **59** (MSSA); **59** (NEGOVURA); **59** (Oliver Hoffmann); **59** (lanych); **64** (Konstantin L); **64** (Pavel Chagochkin); **65** (3DPhoto); **65** (Anton Brand); **65** (Be Good); **65** (cigdem); **65** (dotshock); **66** (Christian Mueller); **67** (MarySan); **67** (alexandre zveiger); **67** (graphixmania); **67** (owatta); **68** (AlexHliv); **68** (Alexapicso); **68** (Didecs); **68** (Katrine Glazkova); **68** (Olga Popova); **68** (shuttersport); **68** (studiovin); **69** (Aroonsak); **70** (Akira Kaelyn); **70** (Denise Kappa); **70** (Petr Malyshev); **70** (TerraceStudio); **71** (s4svisuals); **73** (Ljupco Smokovski); **73** (ivastasya); **73** (kedrov); **75** (Aedka Studio); **76** (Kuziva Shamu); **76** (Olinchuk); **77** (BCFC); **77** (FiledIMAGE); **79** (DenysHolovatiuk); **80** (Crows Nest Factory); **80** (LHF Graphics); **80** (Saint A); **80** (oixxo); **83** (chronicler); **83** (lazyllama); **88** (Nagel Photography); **89** (Paul Hakimata Photography); **91** (artnLera); **93** (Leonard Zhukovsky); **93** (ilikestudio); **100** (Everett Historical); **103** (Natalia Mikhaleva); **104** (Photo Image); **104** (RobertColquhoun); **105** (Alexander Ryabintsev); **113** (Emilian Danaila); **121** (Dark Moon Pictures); **122** (Shmizla); **122** (kamomeen); **124** (JeniFoto); **124** (Texture background wall); **124** (Thoom); **126** (ChristianChan); **127** (Artisticco); **129** (photocritical); **133** (Francesco Abrignani); **136** (DRogatnev); **140** (ShineArt09); **142** (Miss Doreria); **142** (subarashii21); **147** (Anita Ponne); **147** (Anna Kucherova); **147** (Evgeny Atamanenko); **147** (Heath Doman); **147** (Michele Paccione); **147** (mashakotcur); Sue Solie-Patterson (licensed under CC BY-SA 3.0) **122**; Tempo Music School, Dublin: **46**; The Gaiety School of Acting - The National Theatre School of Ireland 1986-2019, Dublin: **46**; The Glasgow Alphabet Map by Rosemary Cunningham. www. illustrationetc.co.uk **106**; Writing.ie **46**; © Dan Gutman **127**; © Lynam school of irish dancing; with the kind permission of Jean Kennedy **47**; © Rimidesigns www.rimidesigns.com.au **6**; © Ron Sumners **93**; ©2012 by Richard Panchyk; Illustration design: Monica Baziuk; All rights reserved including the right of reproduction in whole or in part in any form. This edition published by arrangement with Chicago Review Press c/o Susan Schulman A Literary Agency. Any third party use must be requested directly from Susan Schulman Literary Agency LLC. **128**

Illustrations

Alejandro Milà, Greta Gröttrup

Video

Integra Software Services PVT Ltd, Chennai, Top 10 Things To Do in Dublin Ireland (2015), Alicia Mae Hirté, AMaeTV

Texts

p. 47 from an interview with Jean Kennedy by reporter Siún Lennon, © Siún Lennon; **p. 58** *My Favorite Room* by Edwina Reizer, © Edwina Reizer; **p. 94** from *At Ellis Island: A History in Many Voices* by Louise Peacock, © Atheneum Books for Young Readers; **p. 122** from: *Public School Superheroes* by James Patterson, © Jimmy Patterson Books, Little Brown and Company; **p. 124** *The Story of Saint Patrick* by James A. Janda, © James A. Janda/Paulist Press; **p. 125** from: *If I Built a House* by Chris Van Dusen © Puffin Books; **p. 126** *Back to School Shopping* by Kenn Nesbitt, © Kenn Nesbitt; **p. 127** from: *My Weird School Daze #4* by Dan Gutman, © Harper Collins; **p. 128** adapted from: *New York City History for Kids: From New Amsterdam to the Big Apple with 21 Activities* by Richard Panchyk, © Chicago Review Press.